Trickle Down Mindset

Mindset

The Missing Element In Your Personal Success

BY: MICHAL STAWICKI

www.expandbeyondyourself.com

ISBN: 1507690223
ISBN-13: 978-1507690222

Table of Contents

4

Elusive Success

"There are no stereotypes for success."

— Jim Rohn

The philosopher's stone is a legendary alchemical substance said to be capable of turning base metals such as lead into gold, and to be an elixir of life, useful for rejuvenation and achievement of immortality. For centuries, it was the most sought after goal in alchemy, symbolizing perfection, enlightenment, and heavenly bliss.

And I found it.

Well, not literally. It's not the piece of rock I carry around in my pocket.

It's my personal philosophy. The "trickle down" mindset. You have yours, too, and it may become your personal philosopher's stone. You can turn the ordinary into gold. You can live longer. The effects of your magic factor may last well after your death.

You will achieve the best results if you mingle philosophy with personal development. However, you can see just by looking around, that personal development doesn't seem to be the answer for most folks. Every year there are millions of new personal development books sold and podcasts downloaded. Hundreds and thousands of people attend personal development seminars, and the circulation of *Success* magazine is half a million. But the success stories that we hear of are numbered in the hundreds or thousands at most.

There is a missing element in this puzzle. The method that has brought fame and fortune to some seems to be completely useless or of limited functionality to others. I grasped this dissonance almost as soon as I returned to personal development study following a sixteen-year hiatus.

My personal observations have been that about five percent of personal development students achieve any real success. Jeff Olson, author of *The Slight Edge*, comes to the same conclusion. By "success," I don't mean millions in your bank account, but rather, realizing your personal goals, whatever they are. Saint Mother Teresa of Calcutta wasn't a millionaire. In fact, she lived in conditions regarded as pitiful by the majority of Americans. But I think most of us would agree she was a smashing success.

I carefully studied income disclosures of several multi-level marketing (MLM) companies and the numbers confirm my observations. Those numbers are relevant because the MLM industry relies heavily on personal development. The idea is that with proper training, every "average Joe" can became a millionaire.

So there is a dissonance. Crowds are unsuccessfully trying to tame the elusive art of personal development.

But is this different in other spheres? Do people studying medicine, finance, or entrepreneurship have better results, more success? No. Olson's numbers apply to society in general.

The success stories highlighted as a result of personal development are impressive. However, many people say personal development is a scam. That gurus are preying on the naïveté of crowds. It's the modern equivalent of the "opium of the masses," that positive thinking and affirmations are simply a substitute for hard work.

These are arguments from people that have never tried to practice personal development or who belong to the 95 percent group, people that never saw significant effects as a result of personal development.

And sadly, in most cases, these arguments are valid. If the overall efficiency is the same as in, let's say, the retail industry, the personal development claims sound hollow. All those "magic ingredients" and "secrets to success" supposedly "available to anyone" work against the personal development industry.

The best remedy, then, is to show massive and measurable results, which will quiet the critics. But in order to achieve them, something needs to change in the way students approach personal development. As the reality shows, the past approach has not been optimal. It lacked the stress on student's efforts necessary to make the whole thing work.

To make it work you need a solid personal philosophy.

That philosophy is not restricted to the realm of personal development. Your attitude is important in everything you do, be it in your job, business, education, or relationships. You may disregard personal development as one big scam, but you can still make your life better by fixing your attitude. And by linking your philosophy with a personal development program, you will boost your results.

Look around you and examine the people you meet every day. How many of them are enjoying good health? How many have lasting, strong relationships? How many have unwavering belief and trust in their Creator? How many have financial security? How many are living purposeful lives and are eager to start every day with its various challenges? And most important, how many of them have these simultaneously?

Five percent, more or less. No matter if they consciously practice personal development or not. No matter if they are housewives, CEOs, nurses, programmers, retired soldiers, plumbers, grandfathers, or teachers. And it's because they have a good personal philosophy. It's not something special reserved for special people. Everyone has some worldview and life attitude. You do too.

It's not relevant where are you in your life right now, whether you have a lot of money, are fit or obese, young or old. You have your internal compass that guides you through your existence. In addition, you are equipped with a free will and a conscious mind. You can form and mold your personal philosophy. You can change. It's in your power.

I will go back to this mantra time and again in this book: you define success for yourself, nobody else does. Don't be intimidated by the examples I will share in this book. Most of them are what you could call "stereotypes of success."

You don't need to have a Rolls Royce, a fat bank account, fame, or a lot of friends to consider yourself successful. You define your purpose and you are fulfilled by achieving that purpose. The right personal philosophy allows you to reach it no matter what you will come up with as your life's core.

You will fail miserably without the proper attitude. A successful life is possible only for those who are backed up by a successful personal philosophy. Every single man and woman who has ever been satisfied with his or her life accomplishments had a set of beliefs and convictions, and a guiding internal mechanism that allowed them to do what they've done. Just a handful out of thousands examples:

"I do not think there is any other quality so essential to success of any kind as the quality of perseverance. It overcomes almost everything, even nature."

- John D. Rockefeller

"The major difference isn't circumstance; it's the set of the sail, or the way we think."

- Jim Rohn

"To love until it hurts."

- Mother Teresa of Calcutta

"I shall conquer untruth by truth. And in resisting untruth, I shall put up with all suffering."

- Mahatma Gandhi

> *"The secret of success is learning how to use pain and pleasure instead of having pain and pleasure use you. If you do that, you're in control of your life. If you don't, life controls you."*
>
> - Tony Robbins

> *"No pessimist ever discovered the secret of the stars, or sailed to an uncharted land, or opened a new doorway for the human spirit."*
>
> - Helen Keller

If you don't believe me, then pick a successful person you know. Approach him or her and ask the question: "Where does your success come from?" I bet they won't reply, "Oh, I don't know, it just happened. It's luck, I suppose." Even if they think their success comes from luck, another question will reveal what they consider luck: "Where did your luck come from?" They will tell you about God, internal drive, courage to take chances, or people who supported them.

If you look closely at the examples I mentioned above or if you do a few of these interviews and compare the answers, you will realize there is an irregularity to their answers. Personal philosophies of different people may include a lot of common elements, but they all are unique. Thus, you can borrow the pieces of someone else's philosophies, but only you can shape your successful personal philosophy for yourself.

That's the first characteristic of personal philosophy: it's unique.

The second one is that it's intangible. It's not something you can weigh or measure. It's hidden in your mind and heart. It is shaped by your experiences and interpretation of those experiences.

And that's the problem.

Unfortunately, we as a society went a bit too far in the direction of materialism. We don't trust the intangible. We are afraid that it will elude us, that we will look stupid giving our attention and appreciation to something that cannot be measured, seen, or pinpointed, that we will waste time and effort on something that doesn't really exist.

It's an idiotic attitude, but our society is crammed with it.

Take your mind for an instance. Is it something you can measure? By what? The weight of your brain? Its volume? The number of neural connections? The electrical activity in your brain? All of these metrics are just an approximation of your mind and they are not even close to the description of your ego, your essence.

Read the confused comments on the TED Talk by Angela Lee Duckworth about grit. She and her team researched a vast number of individuals from many different industries and discovered the only common successful trait of all these successful people was grit: an ability to focus on the long-term approach and do the job it takes. And a lot of people have a problem with this because it's intangible and cannot be measured.

In a way, personal philosophy resembles a philosopher's stone—a medium to turn everything into gold (success) and, as a byproduct, giving eternal life.

Like the effect of a mystical philosopher's stone, the way it works is invisible and hard to explain. However, the effects it provides are so spectacular that it's not possible to ignore them. But unlike the philosopher's stone, personal philosophy is within your reach. You don't need to seek magical alchemical formulas to own it. All you need is already inside you.

Tamed Success

"Mental fight means thinking against the current, not with it. It is our business to puncture gas bags and discover the seeds of truth."

— Virginia Woolf

If you know anything about marketing, you know that market research is a must. You need to know that your product, service, or idea is worth pursuing before you commit your resources to developing it. If there are products similar to your own that are selling well, that's a good sign.

The first time I thought about writing this book, I went straight to Amazon.com and typed "personal philosophy" into the search bar. I found over 2800 results in the Kindle store, but most of them were only loosely related to the topic. Those that were laser-focused on it were also the ones that didn't sell very well (more than 600,000 on the Best Sellers List). Then I typed the same search term into Google. Only 1.35 million results ("weight loss" provided 62 million results).

A disappointment. This book will not be profitable. But I decided to write it anyway. I know it will serve many people well. We don't all need to lose weight, but we all need a solid personal philosophy to thrive. It's crucial for achieving success. It's almost as important as food and shelter and I discovered that it's totally neglected!

In a way it reminded me of the research I had done on perseverance. This trait is pointed out by almost every successful businessman, entrepreneur, and sportsman as a vehicle to success. And there are only about seven million search results in Google for that word. However, if you type "success" into the search bar, Google will spit out over 300 million results! Can you imagine? We all desire success, but we also ignore the most obvious way to achieve it.

It's not surprising, then, that less than five percent of people are successful. Actually, in light of the above numbers, it's surprising that this ratio is so high.

Personal philosophy is even more neglected than perseverance, but it is more intrinsic to the output of your life. I need it, you need it, everyone needs it. Someone has to point it out. I decided that this someone may as well be me—Michal Stawicki.

Just in case you don't know Jim Rohn's story, until the age of 25, he was just an average Jim in an obscure part of Idaho. He quit college at nineteen and got a job. After six years, he was not successful at all. He was working hard but was deep in debt nonetheless. And he was unable to change his situation. What could he do? He was just a farm boy. Taxes were high and corrupt politicians didn't much care about common folk. Then he met his mentor and worked in several of his businesses. By 31, he was a millionaire.

Strangely enough, politicians were still corrupt, the average wage hadn't changed much in that period nor had the taxes. Rohn stated, multiple times, that the key factor to his change was his personal philosophy, nothing less and nothing more.

He mastered many different techniques from many different areas of personal development and business: how to chisel your character, how to manage your time, how to set and accomplish your goals, how to stay motivated, how to persevere, how to face failures and draw the conclusions from them among many, many others. But he didn't attribute his life transition to any of those various elements. He considered the change in his personal philosophy as the first and basic reason for his success.

In October 2012, I listened to Darren Hardy's *The Compound Effect*, where he mentioned that Jim was his mentor. I checked out Jim's materials then. I immediately felt a level of familiarity I hadn't felt in any other self-help teacher. I felt like I was listening to the older brother I never had. Almost every word was hitting my heart, my mind, or both.

You have no idea how strongly it affected me when I heard his story for the first time. Until I was 33, I lived the life of an average guy. I once had big dreams, but they hadn't worked out, so I led a mediocre life.

Are you struggling, stressed or frustrated? Don't see a bright future ahead of you? Does it seem like the road to success and happiness eludes you? Do you find consolation in Rohn's story? Can you relate to it?

I hope this will be as big a discovery for you as it was for me. You may be an Idaho farm boy today or today's equivalent—a Starbucks barista. You may have been "the farm boy" for the last several years and you may still be a millionaire several years from now. Or an actor, or a successful entrepreneur, or an author.

Your fate is not set in stone. In fact, it's in your hands and you can chisel it out of fate's matter, like an artist creating a sculpture. If you are on a higher level than Jim was at 25, it's even more encouraging. If he made it, why shouldn't you?

There is hope for you. No matter if you feel like a failure right now or even if you feel moderately successful. No matter if you have been pursuing personal development for years without many results. No matter if you consider self-help something for the naive. An ordinary guy made it. And it's not an isolated story. The same thing happened to Bob Proctor, to Beau Norton, to Michal Stawicki.

The process is repeatable. You can do it too. So, what do you need to make it happen for you? The same thing Jim Rohn considered crucial to his progress: develop the right personal philosophy. And this book will help you to do exactly that.

The Philosopher's Stone

"Alchemy is the process of transforming something common into something special."

— Jason van Orden

You are incredibly lucky! You've just found the philosopher's stone. Thousands of medieval alchemists looked for it in vain for centuries. Now it's within your reach. It is your personal philosophy. It is the single most important factor to your wellbeing and happiness. It's the key to your life and your purpose on this planet. It can transform anything you touch into gold. Mind you, money is not the only indicator of success. Currency represents the multitude of exchanges that take place at any given moment in our society. If you can present your achievements in monetary value, everybody immediately recognize its worth.

For example, my personal philosophy allowed me to shed some fat and become the fittest I have been in my life. I didn't monetize this experience very much. I published a book sharing my experiences, but I priced it at only $1 and after several months, I was able to give the book away for free. I created a free Lift plan and wrote a few articles about weight loss. I didn't make a lot of money from those activities, but being fit and healthy indirectly provided me with thousands of dollars. Because I changed my diet and exercise regime, I had a lot more energy than before. I was able to marry my day job with simultaneously writing and publishing books. For over a year now, I've been working 13+ hours almost every day.

You may be deep in debt or obese, but you need to take care of your mindset first and pursue weight loss or new investment techniques next. Without a philosopher's stone, all your attempts to transform lead into gold are in vain. Assuming you persevere in your quest long enough (which is a bold assumption without the right philosophy), you will surely receive *some* results. But with the right mindset in the first place, those results will multiply.

Ditch other worries. If you are not in the place you'd like to be in your life, focus on fixing your personal philosophy. Do it and you will see results in all other areas as well.

Of course, you may also neglect it. You have free will. What you do with your life is up to you. But neglect developing your personal philosophy and you'll probably doom yourself to a lifelong struggle. If you don't consciously work on your philosophy, it will be developed naturally by external agents: the content you consume, the data input habits you've developed, your past experiences and how they shaped your interpretation of external events, and most important, the people around you.

If you aren't satisfied with your life, I urge you: start working on your personal philosophy immediately. Yes, you can do it. You can learn to govern the way your mindset develops in the same way you learned to govern your hand movements. You decide whether or not to reach for a hamburger or a salad. You can also decide what you read, what you watch, what you listen to, and with whom you spend your time.

Your brain is bombarded with millions of impulses all the time. It is busy interpreting them all the time. You can take control of the natural processes of absorbing and interpreting the outside data.

Of course, it is impossible to consciously examine every smell, color, movement, noise, gesture, and the thousands of other impulses you gather every second. But you can filter them with the net of your beliefs and convictions. You can incrementally model them and influence your personal philosophy that way. It's doable. Your beliefs may be changed when examined by facts.

Initially, I gave my new philosophy a chance, tracked my efforts, and compared the effects against my previous beliefs. I didn't believe I could save more money. I had honed my savings management skills for years. I knew my numbers by heart: the interest rate of my savings, the mortgage rate, the respective monthly cost of food, clothes, medications, and so on. I planned monthly budgets. Then I exposed myself to new ideas and opened my mind enough to try them. Within a few months, my savings rate skyrocketed from 4.5 percent to 20 percent. My beliefs shifted a bit.

So, is developing your personal philosophy something you feel inclined to do? Is it for you? That's for you to answer. I'm just doing my best to encourage you to start. This book is designed for you if you have been struggling with achieving your goals for too long. If book after book, seminar after seminar, has not helped you get what you want, it's time to try something different. If you strive to change, amend your philosophy first.

It is easy to do, like everything else in your life. If you want to write a book, its creation depends on thousands of keystrokes. Each single keystroke is easy to do. However, it's also easy to not do.

Chiseling your personal philosophy depends on multitudes of tiny decisions: Averting your eyes from the TV when you cross the living room or sitting on the couch for five minutes. Spending five minutes gossiping, or reading a blog post. Saying a short prayer or numbing your mind playing video games. Each decision depends on your will. Each is made now. You aren't facing an infinite number of decisions. They are in your future. All you need *now* is to make a single, simple, tiny decision. It's in your power.

Should you give it a try? Tell me, what do you have to lose? Only your old lousy personal philosophy, which hasn't served you very well so far. You risk becoming someone else: someone more successful, someone more fulfilled, someone who is doing more for themselves, the community, and the world. If you have some reservations about transforming into someone else, think about Jim Rohn's story. Do you really think one more farm boy struggling to stay afloat for the rest of his life would be a better thing for the world? Or in your opinion, did he choose well pursuing something more?

In the end, you are the only person who can answer all these questions.

Knowledge Items:

- If you strive to change, amend your philosophy first. *examine your values first*
- It's as easy to do, as to neglect.

Philosophy Defined

"Worthless people live only to eat and drink; people of worth eat and drink only to live."

— Socrates

What is a personal philosophy?
For now, this simplistic definition is enough: *"A system a person forms for conduct of life."*

I will go deeper into this later on.

Now let's consider what this definition implies. It applies to a person, a human being. If you are one, you qualify.

Everyone has a personal philosophy. We are constructed that way. No matter if you are a CEO of a Fortune 500 company or a housewife and mother of six. It's an integral part of human construction. It's not even like a kidney or leg, which you can live without. And just as having a leg or kidney is not an indication of success, the same is true with personal philosophy. Rockefeller had his own and a couch potato also has his own, which states: "I value beer, TV, and my couch more than anything else in my life." This sentence is at his core and dictates his thoughts and actions. It shapes who he is.

"Conduct of life" is not some gimmick, a smart technique, or a trick you can pull out of your sleeve and use to improve a specific situation. The right personal philosophy will help you in all of life's situations. The wrong one will hinder you.

And it's a system, "a set of principles or procedures according to which something is done; an organized scheme or method." It's not karma or magic. It's not fate or destiny beyond your influence. Like every system, it has a set of rules.

I consider that personal philosophy's system to consist of your *past experiences* and *their interpretation* in your mind, plus your *input sources* and *an internal interpretation* of them.

These are *the only* things in the universe you need to work on to change your future. The only things you really have the power over. Change your input sources, change the interpretation you give to the incoming data, and it will change you.

The definition says that a person "forms" her philosophy. You do it all the time and have been doing it almost since you were born. You have your senses and they are constantly absorbing information. You process the data and give it meaning all the time. Your existence itself utilizes those components. It is as natural as breathing.

Your essence, your thoughts, and actions are also dictated by your philosophy, the way you conduct your life. Yet, it's overlooked.

Have you heard of this concept before? Maybe, if you were studying personal development diligently. Did you know the definition of personal philosophy prior to reading this book? Then you are a part of an elite minority.

But hearing about it is not uncommon. Even realizing the concept on your own is not such a big deal. All in all, it is like using logic to draw the conclusion that air is indispensable for humans and that we are all equipped with lungs to utilize it.

However, here comes another, less obvious question: Did you consciously form your system for conduct of life? Did you try to leverage it to get more of what you consider important in life? If you really did, then I'm surprised you are reading this book. Because it seems that people who do this are enormously successful and satisfied.

As you can see just by browsing the titles of self-help books, we don't usually seek methods to fix our whole lives. When something hurts us, we react and look for the solution for that particular pain: how to have more time, money, use them better, get fit, look well, and so on.

And you are probably not much different than the majority. You've never thought that if you created a specific mindset, you would get all of that and more.

What usually sells are solutions to our problems, remedies to our pain. A brilliant time management system, motivational system, goal-setting system, and so on. But people fail in applying that advice because they don't possess an efficient internal system to conduct their lives.

My blunt theory is that the personal development industry took this approach for one of two reasons:

1. They care only about money.

People who produce such materials don't care about the real effectiveness of their programs. Application of their teachings depends solely on their customers. They pay and don't get the results? Who cares? Nobody coerced them to reach into their wallets. They are probably losers anyway if they can't utilize such a brilliant system.

2. They assume that the question of personal philosophy is already answered.

Most people who provide personal development content are practitioners. They don't theorize much. They either are not aware of their successful personal philosophy or they take for granted that anyone who is attempting to improve his or her life is doing it with the right attitude. But assumptions are dangerous animals. If not tended to properly, they bite. And a lot of people get involved in studying personal development, while only a handful see tangible results from their studies.

I'm fully convinced that a lot more people would get better results if the focus were put on the personal philosophy first and on various different techniques later on. You can see this if you take a look at the personal development bestselling book lists. Books that are focused on the timeless principles and the right mindset are forever alive: *Meditations* by Marcus Aurelius; *The 7 Habits of Highly Effective People*, by Stephen R. Covey; *The*

Slight Edge, by Jeff Olson; *Think and Grow Rich*, by Napoleon Hill; *As A Man Thinketh* by James Allen; and *Man's Search for Meaning* by Victor Frankl. Other books, which ignore the question of mindset or don't treat it seriously enough, are gradually forgotten. Why? They don't provide the results, not because the programs they contain are trash, but because people with average personal philosophies can achieve only average results.

The human brain is a gigantic filtering mechanism. You register 100 million impulses from your senses every second. Your brain remembers every single image, sound, smell, and body sensation you experience throughout your life. Your memory capacity is practically infinite. But in order to keep our feeble conscious mind sane, the part of the brain called the reticular formation filters out more than 99 percent of those memories. This way your ego is not overloaded with the raw data and can focus on higher-level activities like abstract thinking.

What penetrates your conscious mind is the carefully chosen set of data that your brain thinks is relevant to you or crucial for your survival. For example, sudden noise has a wide motorway reserved for your filtering mechanism. It almost always goes through filters and causes an automatic fear reaction.

Think of this mechanism as a board of directors presenting a carefully chosen set of data to their CEO. You are the smart CEO and your brain is the pack of dumb managers. They provide you with the data they expect will be of interest to you. For example, if a CEO is a profit-driven, they won't hassle him with the "unimportant" data about employees' (dis)satisfaction levels. However, they will readily present him the marketing and sales data. It's not that the managers don't know or don't care about huge employee rotation rates. They were taught by their CEO in the past that that kind of information didn't interest him. If he asks for that data, though, they will readily provide it.

Your brain is doing the same thing. It took all your up-to-date life experiences, emotions, and thoughts and put them into your personal philosophy, your "system for conduct of life." And it provides you with the data that's in accordance with this philosophy.

Only if you start asking different questions will you get different answers. You must ask your board of directors for methods suitable for improving your life, and you must do it with the proper attitude. Not: "Why this is happening to me?" but "How can I use it to my advantage?"

Knowledge Items:

- *Personal philosophy is a system a person forms for conduct of life*
- *Everyone has one.*
- *People with an average personal philosophy can achieve only average results.*

It's Personal

"The more you like yourself, the less you are like anyone else, which makes you unique."

— Walt Disney

Your personal philosophy is your most individual piece of reality. It's more unique to you than your genotype. The way you gather information and interpret it is unique. You can live in the same place, have the same family, experience the same hardships as any other person, but you give them your own meaning.

Les Brown and his twin brother, Wesley, had almost identical data inputs in early childhood. But only one of them became a world-class speaker. We observe this throughout history—people who live in the same ghetto achieve radically different end results.

However, it's not the external circumstances, but what you do with them that counts. It's not the resources, but your resourcefulness, which dictates your life's outcome. You are responsible for the end result, not the society, not your neighborhood or family. Those are just the resources and data sources you were given. However, you must actually use them to create something admirable out of your story.

This belief, that every individual is solely responsible for their own life, is, by the way, one of the pillars of many successful individuals' personal philosophies. I'll be referring back to this later on.

Now, let's talk about your own personal philosophy. In order to mold it, you first need to accept that you have one and it is inseparable from your essence. If you fix those two facts in your conscious mind, it will be possible to move on and actually change your personal philosophy. If you acknowledge these facts, then the road to new opportunities will open up. If you deny them, it's unlikely you will achieve lasting change.

I have read more than 50 books on personal development. Only a handful of them had a profound impact on my life. The difference between the information that changed my life and the information that didn't was simple: I either rejected or accepted and took ownership of the ideas presented in the books I had read. It's not the information, but how I digested and implemented it that made the difference. The most vivid example is *The 7 Habits of Highly Effective People* by Stephen R. Covey. I read this book for the first time when I was about 17. I found it interesting. And not much changed in my life as a result of reading it.

The next time I read it was in October 2012. This time I took its teachings straight to heart because I accepted the message of the book as my own. Because I saw that it is true in my life too, I took action. I wrote my personal mission statement in November 2012 and my life was changed forever.

I became an author. My savings ratio skyrocketed from 4.5 percent of my income to 20 percent. I lost weight and, at 35, I'm the fittest I have ever been in my life. I passed three professional exams and got two certificates in my day job field of expertise. I ditched my vices: playing computer games, watching TV, and excessively reading popular novels. I started to pray twice as much as before. I developed about 40 new daily habits. I could see my personal mission statement materializing in front of my eyes.

It was the same book I had read 18 years ago, but it generated a totally different outcome. The information in the book didn't change one iota. Only my reception of it did.

A personal philosophy is a powerful tool for progress and growth that can change your life for the better, starting right here and now. But you can't treat it as a tidbit or an interesting theory. Embrace the concept, make it your own, and you will become an invincible weapon.

So let's get back to you. Do you believe you have your own personal philosophy? Do you own your system for conduct of life?

The answer should be obvious because you are alive, and you are somehow conducting your life in every minute. What's your system? Ponder this question for a few minutes.

How do you react to specific kinds of events?

What situations make you comfortable and which stress you out?

For whom do you feel love and for whom do you feel hostility?

Do you realize any patterns in your answers? A system that lurks behind them?

If you didn't just skip the above questions then I assume you reached the conclusion that you have some kind of personal philosophy. It's kind of obvious, I know, like asking you to raise your hand to reach the conclusion that you have an arm. But sometimes we don't see the obvious. It appears that the matter of personal philosophy is one of the things we take for granted and don't give enough attention.

Do you know where your personal philosophy came from?

The short answer is "life."

It was shaped by every data input and every personal interpretation you gave to that data. Everything you smelled, saw, or heard had some impact on your present state of mind. Every meaning you assigned to those impulses was also important. Sometimes meanings you didn't assign had an impact, too. Whatever you have repeatedly ignored is more likely to be ignored by your brain in the future. Your every experience and every interaction subtly formed your present mindset.

Try to distill your current personal philosophy to make you more familiar with the concept on a very personal level. How? Simply take a look at your present actions. Your actions are determined by the way you see yourself and the world. In other words, they are determined by your personal philosophy.

Analyze your actions and you will find the beliefs driving them. The same goes for your inactions.

Conduct an honest review of your actions. And please, don't make excuses. "I can't do it, because…" or "when I will have this, then…" Nick Vujicic has no limbs, but he doesn't need excuses. He could lie in a bed for the rest of his life and rightfully claim he is disabled and needs help, but he doesn't. So let's make a contract: you can start using excuses as soon as you do at least as much as Nick has done with his life.

I was able to reverse engineer my previous personal philosophy by analyzing my past actions. In a nutshell, that previous philosophy said, *"Do just enough to get by and try to enjoy the rest of the time."* I worked just to get the money to live off. My jobs offered no progress or social acceptance. I did my duty as a father and husband, the head of the family, but as soon as I could, I ducked out and played on the computer or read. I was moderately responsible, but whenever I had a choice between an obligation and entertainment, I chose the entertainment.

Make an inventory of your actions and ponder what they say about your philosophy. I know you would prefer an out-of-the-box solution. I would prefer it too. But the problem with quick fixes is that they fix you quickly, but only when you are already fixed. You know, the whole "when the student is ready, the master appears" thing.

Of course, you could get some great results from any given how-to solution. Action almost always beats inaction. It's better to try something new and fail than not change your behavior and expect that the change will materialize on its own. Besides, everything affects everything. If you get some results from such a program, you will get different input, a different interpretation of facts, which in turn will shift your personal philosophy a bit. A tangible result will have an effect on your intangible attitude.

But we already established that such an approach has only about a five percent success rate. I consider such a percentage ineffective.

So, what should you do?

The only person who can answer this question is you. My advice really comes down to this: read this book, ponder it, digest its message, and most of all, make this message your own. Only then, act upon it. That's the sole universal "quick fix" you will ever find in personal development materials. Your personal philosophy determines what you accept from this and every other book. That's why you should work more on yourself than on any external material.

Your philosophy is unique. And no single entity in the universe, including God Himself, can influence your philosophy without your consent. That's how humans are created and that's how they function. Even if I wanted to implant my beliefs in you, I can't do that.

The magic component of any activity that has the goal of improving your life is YOU.

What works for YOU. What YOU can apply. How YOU can change. What are YOUR values? You, you, you, and YOU! All I'm trying to achieve via this book is to help you to change your life.

I can assure you that you are capable of doing this. I have done so and so have others. We are not freaks who did impossible things unattainable to ordinary mortals. On the contrary, we used ordinary mortal powers to achieve the results each of us is capable of.

Find your own path.

Create your own personal philosophy. I can't do this for you. Only you can unlock your real potential.

The most widely known advocate of the personal philosophy concept was Jim Rohn, but you don't need to be his clone to harness the power of personal philosophy. You don't need the kind of money or hardships he had. You don't need to be raised in a similar background. You don't even need to have the positive character traits he possessed. Well, at least you don't need them at the beginning. All you need is to form your personal philosophy and mold it so it will generate the desired output: money, health, or appropriate traits. Whatever suits your definition of success.

Knowledge Items:

- *Your personal philosophy is more unique to you than your genotype.*
- *YOU have one and it is inseparable from your essence.*
- *It's not the information, but how you digest and implement it that makes the difference.*

A Deeper Look

"If you've reached the point in life where you feel you've got all the answers, you better start asking some different questions."

— Jim Rohn

We dealt with the "personal" part of your philosopher's stone. Now it's time for the second part. According to the Oxford Dictionary, philosophy is:

1. the study of the fundamental nature of knowledge, reality, and existence, especially when considered as an academic discipline.
a particular system of philosophical thought.
plural noun: philosophies
"the philosophies of Plato and Aristotle"
the study of the theoretical basis of a particular branch of knowledge or experience.
"the philosophy of science"
synonyms: thinking, reasoning, thought, wisdom, knowledge
"a lecturer in philosophy"
2. a theory or attitude that acts as a guiding principle for behavior.

The etymology of a word says more about the concept than the present definition of it. Philosophy is derived from "knowledge, body of knowledge," from the old French *filosofie* and directly from Latin *philosophia* and from Greek *philosophia*, "love of knowledge, pursuit of wisdom; systematic investigation," where *philo* means "loving" and *sophis* means "wise, learned."

As you can see, this book is a bit skewed towards the second definition, but instead of particular behavior, it focuses on your life as a whole. It is also worth noting that one of the primary meanings of philosophy in the ancient world was "systematic investigation."

Your personal philosophy is your life attitude formed by your all past experiences and the meanings you gave them. And *it can be systematically investigated and developed using the reasoning faculties of your mind.*

Do you see how the definition of philosophy almost automatically makes your present world view a personal philosophy? Your life experience is your knowledge and wisdom mixed and distilled into philosophy. You are designed to function this way, that's how your brain operates. It gets the input, registers it, examines it, and saves the results. A child who touched a hot kettle received the input and gave it meaning—"hot kettles hurt" —and then formed a piece of philosophy that informed him how to conduct his life—"avoid hot kettles."

We all need such a frame of reference to operate without information overload. You would go crazy if you needed to approach every fact like a scientist examining a new object. Extrapolating a general conclusion based on a few pieces of data from your past allows you to free up your brain capacity for higher functions.

A myriad of inputs and meanings form your way of thinking about the world and your role in it. And this way of thinking determines what actions you undertake.

Okay. I hope you've grasped how absolutely fundamental your personal philosophy is to your life. **It's the filter for everything you encounter and the generator of everything you do.** It's your sanity shield and action engine. Once you realize the importance of your personal philosophy, you can't stop yourself from finding ways to improve it.

If you are not convinced about this, go back to the previous chapter and try to embrace this concept on a personal and emotional level. Because if you don't, then the rest of this book may be interesting, but won't change your life.

So to achieve tangible results you need to change your intangible thinking process. Borrowing other's ideas won't help much unless you make those ideas your own.

But is it possible to absorb a "foreign" way of thinking? Absolutely. What you consider your personal philosophy, your self-image, and your worldview is likely to be just a conglomerate of your parents', your siblings', your friends', and respected authorities' personal philosophies. You automatically absorbed their belief systems trying to sort out this complicated world of ours. Your brain loves generalization. If mommy said that talking to strangers is dangerous and you hadn't any data conflicting this point of view, you just saved that information for further reference and made it part of your operating system. One more puzzle piece had been classified and your brain could put a bit more power into solving other puzzles or enjoying the present moment.

A basic prerequisite to absorbing bits of others' philosophies is to know them. You can't make something your own if you've never heard of it. So your first task is to seek new sources of data inputs. If you never watch TV, turn it on (and recognize that useful philosophies are generally absent there. Well, that's my opinion; form your own). If you watch TV every day, turn it off and go out. If you don't remember the last time you read a book, start reading one. If you read fiction, start reading nonfiction. If you don't read magazines, read a few issues. If you are religious, read an agnostic's blog post. If you are an atheist, go to church.

Break your routine, do something new. Look for new people to meet. Find data sources different to those that shaped your existing philosophy, which doesn't serve you well enough. Approach new things with an open mind. Don't sabotage your physical attempts (new places, new people, new sources of ideas) using your mental terrorists: distrust, arrogance, and reluctance.

Knowledge Items:

- You can systematically investigate and develop your personal philosophy using the reasoning faculties of your mind.
- Borrowing other's ideas won't help much unless you make those ideas your own.

Action Items:

- *Start by breaking your routine by using different data sources or meeting new people.*

Question Your Beliefs

"First say to yourself what you would be; and then do what you have to do."

— Epictetus

In April 2014, I read *Catalyst*, which argued using solid scientific research that confidence is the mysterious, hard to define, but game-changing factor that "reacts with our strengths, shapes what we achieve and who we become."

They described in detail how overconfidence becomes aggression and lack of confidence makes you an underdog. They also gave some very convincing examples on how having steady, well-grounded confidence can have a positive impact on every aspect of your life.

And they were right. Real, heartfelt confidence is a game changer. A person who knows their worth and acts with steadfast confidence will achieve more and become more. However, they didn't take into account where the confidence is born. It starts in your mind.

Confidence doesn't just automatically happen when you know you are right or strong or experienced. Besides, if you are like most people, you rarely allow yourself such thoughts and beliefs. Doubt and hesitation are more likely to preoccupy your mind. You need a solid set of beliefs supported by your experiences to draw confidence from. In other words, you need the right personal philosophy.

If part of your personal philosophy is the belief that people are generally selfish and strive for "I win, you lose" situations, you cannot act with confidence. Confidence is acting with trust, as the etymology of the word shows. You may be an expert in your field and have long years of experience that should support your self-confidence, but with such a philosophy, you are doomed to fail.

One of the aspects of your worldview is how it affects every new input you receive. Personal philosophy filters the ideas you are exposed to. It works almost like a conscious counterpart of reticular formation in your brain. Your whole being depends on how your brain processes external information. It constantly registers, analyzes, and saves every sensory input and abstract concept. You must absolutely trust your most basic coping mechanism to maintain your mind's integrity (read: sanity). You can't constantly doubt your every past experience, memory, or belief.

Your brain is lazy. It doesn't enjoy the mysteries of the universe. It prefers to stay dormant, without any challenging ideas. It avoids thinking as much as possible. Hence, it does everything in its power to stop you from facing a cognitive dissonance. And rightfully so. It can threaten the stability of your personality. Unfortunately, in our age, the brain overdoes this function, defending you not only against revolutionary ideas but also against a fuller life.

If your present philosophy doesn't serve you well, you should get new data sources and interpret the data from a new perspective. If you are a believer and read an atheist's post for the first time in years, beware the attitude "he is a moron; I know better." If you are an atheist and went to church for the first time since you were a teenager, don't judge the people there as "cretins, who are talking with the figments of their imagination." Those are your old convictions and they don't introduce a new perspective. They just create a mental firewall against new ideas. If someone who preaches a different point of view is a moron or a cretin, then you are not obliged to pay attention to his jabbering, are you? And instead of probing the new philosophies, you will just consolidate your present one.

Your set of beliefs is filtering the ideas you come into contact with, labeling them, and discarding the vast majority of them, which are not well aligned with your present philosophy. These conflicting ideas are just simply ignored most of the time. That's why they don't challenge your existing beliefs. Your brain loooooooves coziness and laziness. This mode of operation allows it to dispose of adversaries before they even show up.

The other magic your brain does to maintain your status quo is to interpret things. It is trying to interpret all the events, experiences, and feedback from others in a way that amplifies your existing philosophy. Think of the issue of global warming. Did you heard of the infamous Climategate? The scientists who believed that the rise of the average temperature correlates with human activity tried to ignore data that contradicted their vision or interpreted it in a way that was in accordance with their views, which is what your brain does automatically.

To maintain your cognitive integrity, the brain literally disrupts reality. In the same way global warming believers extended the date range to fit their worldview, your brain receives a bit of reality and grinds it into a pulp that is familiar to you. You are a Democrat and a Republican politician did something right? He had some ulterior motive for sure! You are in the union and you've heard that some corporation gave their employees in China an unexpected bonus? Ha, they felt guilty, that's why!

Your brain pulls out every trick, uses any excuse to maintain the status quo. It doesn't care much about logic. It can be employed to your advantage. You can use logic and reasoning to dismantle such a flawed philosophy and install a better one in its place. I would even argue that falsifying the evidence is your brain's last resort. It has more subtle ways to distort reality. The most powerful one is cutting you out from the sources of input that it considers to be dangerous to your existing philosophy. Is this periodical a Republican mouthpiece? Don't read it. Is this TV station Democrat-friendly? Don't watch it. Turn your attention to the "right" sources, the ones that fully agree with your mentality.

By picking up the data inputs for you, it avoids the cognitive dissonance. You "know" that they preach idiotic ideas in the media, so you skip them. You "know" which media tells the truth, so you consume its content. Simple, but effective. The lazy brain doesn't spend an ounce of effort to fight off the cognitive dissonance; it saves you the precious energy.

Knowledge Items:

- *Your brain constantly interprets all the events, experiences, and feedback from others in a way that amplifies your existing philosophy.*

Action Items:

- *Examine the media you consume AND those you don't. What's your reasoning behind these choices?*

Choose Your Story

"I know how to learn anything I want to learn. I absolutely know that I could learn how to fly the space shuttle because someone else knows how to fly it, and they put it in a book. Give me the book, and I do not need somebody to stand up in front of the class."

— Will Smith

So far, personal philosophy looks like a cure for every human suffering. It sounds too good to be true, doesn't it? You may regard it as some intangible, half-mystical thing of the mind. But where are the tangible results? If this theoretical concept is so effective, it should have at least a small number of real case studies where it was implemented and delivered the results. So where are they?

Everywhere. Every single person who overcame her obstacles and hardships in any area of her life did so because of the shift in her personal philosophy.

Bob Proctor worked at a service station for the fire department. He was in debt and had no hope for the future. He met a mentor who helped him to change his worldview and his life changed dramatically within a single year. He went from earning $4k a year to being an owner of an international company.

Sophie Bennett was broke. She lived a life beyond her means for too long. When she was forced to sell her car, she decided to change. Within seven years, she was a millionaire.

J.K. Rowling was a single mother with no evidence that her story about a boy who discovers his magical heritage was great material for a children's book. But her personal philosophy drove her actions. She didn't quit after the first or fourth rejection.

Beau Norton discovered that his thoughts were creating his reality. His negative thinking was creating a reality that was also negative. His mindset slowly shifted to being more optimistic about life as he learned ways to improve himself. He started an online business and was able to quit his day job at the factory.

People often blame circumstances for their fate. You may be guilty of this bad habit too, if you are not very different from the rest of society. But look at the stories above. Struggles, hardships, and obstacles didn't defeat those people. The external events and circumstances didn't magically change in a moment. The only thing that changed at the beginning was their perspective. Their personal philosophy.

And you can see that it's true in your surroundings, too. I'm sure you know someone who changed his or her life. Whether it was a successful business owner who had gone bankrupt, a young girl who launched a successful business after college, an alcoholic who managed to quit drinking, a recidivist who began an honest life after his last sentence, a woman who pulled herself together following a divorce, or an old man who lost 100 pounds. All these changes are the result of a change in personal philosophy.

If you have an opportunity to talk to someone you know that transformed his or her life, I encourage you to do so and track the changes he or she noticed in the way they thought or interpreted external events.

As with everything else, a personal philosophy may empower an individual or rob him of his power. "Failure stories" also have their origins in personal philosophy.

Again, look around you. I'm sure you can think of some person you know well who is not in the exact place they wish to be in life. You want to convince yourself that this personal philosophy theory is not just a theory, but truth. So the more vivid the example you choose, the easier it will be to notice that internal philosophy, not external circumstances, drives one's actions and the outcomes.

Take the worst drunk, the worst ladies' man, the poorest guy you know. How could it be that his neighbors, from the same district or country achieved a totally different quality of life? Hadn't they similar dysfunctional families? Didn't they attend the same schools?

Where the circumstances are similar, the only explanation for the differences is the human factor. A personal philosophy. Think of Jim Rohn's, Sophie Bennett's, or Bob Proctor's stories. Weren't their peers in very similar situations, coming from very similar backgrounds? But only they became millionaires.

Don't the vast majority of people struggle to keep their heads above water? How many of them do you think will become millionaires? If it all comes down to external factors, if the power of the mind is not important, then all of them are in an excellent starting position to become millionaires. However, the power of mind does matter. It's the only reason those role models succeeded while their peers didn't.

In fact, you are probably better suited for success than they were. If you have a college education, you are ahead of Jim and Bob. If you are not sinking in debt, you are ahead of Sophie Bennett. If you have ever published a short story, you are ahead of J.K. Rowling. According to a pervasive opinion—that external events and circumstances determine your fate—you should become a millionaire sooner rather than later.

But it's a false opinion. It's only when you change your internal structure, the way you observe the world, process information, and interpret that information, that you gain power. It's that simple.

The main difference between successful and unsuccessful philosophies lies in the attitude toward yourself and the world. If you perceive the world as a place of struggle and yourself as a victim of your past, the society you live in, or the job you have, you are closing yourself, preventing yourself from change. On the other hand, if you feel responsible for your actions and their results, if you believe the world was created to serve you not to oppress you, then you are willing to come out of your comfort zone to seek new clues and ideas. Comfort zones and complacency are the allies of failure. Openness and the ability to step out of your comfort zone are signs of success.

I experienced this firsthand. Before my life transformation, I considered myself a partial success at most. I had managed to graduate from a good university, to start and support my family, to develop my spiritual life further than my closest relatives, to keep in reasonably good shape for a white-collar worker. But all of those small successes in different areas were not driving me ahead but rather keeping me in one place. I was almost satisfied with what I had achieved and I was scared that I could lose it. Lose my job, lose my wife, lose my faith.

I lived with feelings of inadequacy and insecurity. I didn't dare to dream big, so I didn't look for sources of new ideas or points of view. To avoid mulling about my experiences, I deadened myself with a hefty dose of computer games and fiction reading. I preferred to spend my time in fictional worlds rather than doing something about the real one.

All of this was happening because my personal philosophy was wrong. I wanted more from life, but I wasn't willing to pay the price. I wished for more resources, but I didn't believe I was capable of getting and keeping them. Hence, I was withholding myself from reaching outside my comfort zone. In order to soothe those conflicting desires, I chose entertainment over work, amusement over discipline.

As you can see, this mix of conflicting ideas wasn't moving me forward. It was a source of constant struggle and frustration. That personal philosophy was only enforcing those negative emotions and I saw almost no positive results.

On the other hand, after my transformation and the shift in my mindset, everything seemed to be more fulfilling. I had the same job, the same apartment (while writing this book I bought my first house), the same long commute, and I burdened myself with dozens of new disciplines. It should have been less comfortable and enjoyable. But it was the opposite. I took joy in practicing my disciplines. I love to write or interact with other bloggers. And, most important, I see the results. I've changed my attitude and I've changed the outputs I got from my actions. Six published titles. A few thousand visits on my blog. Comments and emails from my readers. My English has improved. I achieved my target weight. And so on, and so on. I'm less comfortable, but happier.

The crucial issue in amending your personal philosophy is to import, digest, and assimilate the bits of others' philosophies as your own. Listening to millionaires is hard for non-millionaires. Sometimes they sound like they live in a totally different world. For the common folk, many of their teachings seem to consist mainly of wishful thinking or of assertions that are just not true: "there is abundance for everybody," "you are 100 percent responsible for everything that happens in your life." You see in the news children starving in Africa, so where is this abundance? You lost an arm in a car accident because some drunken jerk decided to drive straight at you. How the heck are you responsible for that?

Abundance and responsibility are suddenly not so compelling when you ponder such facts, are they? But when you overcome this internal resistance, when you stop judging and embrace such attitudes as your own, they start to make sense. But first you need to assimilate them into your worldview. They must be yours to believe them and to start acting upon them.

Different cultures and people find different ways to express the same ideas and beliefs. Take the Catholic faith for an instance. The liturgy in the center of the African continent is different than in Poland or Ireland. The core beliefs are the same, but the way they are expressed through dance or song is different. You also need to incorporate foreign ideas into your internal realm in a unique way. You must believe, or to put it more strongly, you must know that those ideas are true for you and your life.

In the *New Psycho-Cybernetics*, Maltz Maxwell gives multiple instances of the power of belief over reality. He was a plastic surgeon. Many times, changing his patients' physiognomy changed their relation to themselves. But he also met people who looked in the mirror after the operation and said that they didn't see any difference. Their internal self-image was stronger than the image they saw with their own eyes. Those people were hypnotized by their faulty self-image. Under hypnosis, people can do extraordinary things or cannot do the simplest activities. Shy people can become bold and strong men cannot raise their hands from the table. The difference lies in what their minds perceived as truth. If the hypnotist convinced them they were bold or weak, they acted accordingly.

You may be able to do the 'impossible' or be unable do the 'possible.' It depends entirely on what you consider true. That's the reason you need to accept foreign ideas as your own. You simply can't achieve the same things other can because your beliefs stop you from trying.

You must believe that the idea is true before you act upon that idea.

You must open up to it, wrestle with it, ponder it, and if necessary, modify it. Then you can accept it. Once accepted, it becomes a part of your system of conduct of life. Only then can it start to generate different actions and different results.

That's the explanation regarding the phenomenon of people attending the same seminar, reading the same book, or participating in the same course. Those who succeeded embraced the new ideas. Those who didn't change their way of thinking didn't achieve different outputs in their lives. That's why the attitude of the majority of successful people is characterized by open-mindedness.

One of my friends is a top expert in the field of computer networks; he is in the top 1 percent in the world. He has numerous professional certificates and earns a lot more than me. I've known him since childhood. He has a very scientific mind. He worked at a university for several years before pursuing a career in the private sector. He is very down-to-earth. But when I talk with him about the Law of Attraction or some experiments about the impact of the conscious mind on physical reality, he doesn't react with skepticism or disbelief. All he earnestly says is, "It's outside of my field of expertise. It may be true. I don't have enough data to confirm or reject the idea." That's a successful attitude.

Knowledge Items:

- *Every success and failure story has its origin in an individual's personal philosophy.*
- *Comfort zones and complacency are the allies of failure. Openness and ability to step out of your comfort zone are signs of success.*
- *You must believe that the idea is true before you act upon that idea.*

Action Items:

- *Choose a person you know whom you consider a success in a given area. Why do you think this person is successful? Was it luck, talent, upbringing, character, physical resources? Really? Don't you know other people in this area who had the same or more yet didn't perform as well as your role model?*
- *Choose a person you know whom you consider a failure in a given area. Perform investigation similar to that above.*

The Law of Nature

"Failure is a few errors in judgment repeated every day.
Success is a few simple disciplines practiced every day."

— Jim Rohn

There are laws of nature, but we are able to overstep the universe's boundaries. We are not birds, but we can fly. We are not fish, but we can travel through the oceans. We are not polar bears, but we can live in the North.

However, it's not enough to want to overcome nature. We need to spend an incredible amount of conscious effort to achieve it. It may be very easy to buy a plane ticket, pack several things, sit on the plane, and fly to another place, but there are thousands, if not millions of man-hours supporting this simple act. The hours inventors spent on figuring out the concept of putting man in the air; the hours engineers spent developing the technical details; the hours workers spent in the manufacturing plants; the hours the pilot spent on learning his craft; the hours the technical crew spent on maintaining the plane etc.

And all a bird needs to do is flap its wings.

This reveals another law of nature: Whatever you do, whatever you spend your time on, you excel at it. This law applies to animals too and even plants. But they just do what they were created to do. They excel at survival, finding food, seeking a mate, cooperating in a pack and so on. Fish excel at swimming and birds at flying. I don't know if they chose to do this because they are best suited for those tasks or they just followed their instincts blindly. The fact is that they spent their time doing those activities and they excel at them.

You can choose what you will excel at by choosing how you spend your time. If you spend it griping and complaining you will become a master griper and complainer. If you spend it writing, you will become an excellent writer. It's as simple as that.

The definition of the law of nature is "a generalization that describes recurring facts or events in nature."

For example, the laws of thermodynamics are the laws of nature. Have you ever seen an object whose temperature was raised on its own without the energy input from an external source? I don't think so.

Have you seen someone who repeatedly made small errors in judgment and became successful in that particular area? I don't think so.

You might have observed something like this because we can defy the laws of nature. However, we usually achieve this by utilizing other laws. Human cannot fly on their own, but the use of aerodynamic laws means we can soar into the sky.

There are serious testimonials from people who claim to have levitated. The Catholic Church reports that saints were able to do so. Does it mean the laws of gravity didn't apply to them? I don't think so. We just cannot explain right now how it happened. I'm quite sure that there is some underlying "law of sainthood," which allowed them to soar nonetheless.

The law of errors and disciplines in normal circumstances applies to everybody. CEOs and the unemployed, fathers and kids, saints and sinners. What does this have to do with the subject at hand? Simply put, I think you should take this into account when developing your personal philosophy. It would not be sensible to forget about it any more than it would be sensible to forget about gravity.

You are of course free to construct your own philosophy in any way you wish. For example, your financial management may come down to, "I'll keep buying lottery tickets and someday I'll get lucky." Savings and earnings may not be included in such a philosophy. However, the chances of actually making such a strategy a success are easy to count. It's one in many millions. Your personal philosophy may ignore the law of errors and disciplines and still bring you to the point you desire. The chances for that are just very, very tiny. Minuscule.

Any personal philosophy that doesn't take this law into account is flawed. That's why it's important to develop the right habits. They determine how you spend your time, your life. They drive your actions. And in the end, they culminate in your life's achievements.

Small errors repeated over time become our bad habits. Tiny disciplines repeated over time become good ones. NO Small errors and disciplines determine *much* in life. They are applicable to every single area of life—health, wealth, spiritual life, relationships, happiness, education. You won't find a single exception. Jeff Olson made those two statements the core of *The Slight Edge*.

What is so special about this book is that Jeff framed its core message into a practical life philosophy. It made his book a bestseller. It is one of the personal development books that focus on foundations not on pep talks or fancy techniques. He didn't start a marketing campaign. He just passed it on to a few close friends. They in turn did the same to their friends. And more people kept asking to read it. *The Slight Edge* turned out to hold a solution for many people because it helped common people improve their lives.

The first edition was available for purchase only via a 1-800 line, and people kept calling and ordering it. So Jeff kept improving the book. The most recent edition (November 2013) includes the stories of readers who transformed their lives thanks to upgrading their personal philosophies with *The Slight Edge* philosophy elements. These testimonials confirm that this is not a fancy theory presented by millionaires to explain their success. Average, common folks who live in accordance with this law are getting results. Your action doesn't have to be perfect or grand to help you achieve what you want. It just needs to lead you in the right direction and be consistent.

I'm one of those "average Joes" whose stories are included in *The Slight Edge*. Reading it, I realized that this law is true and I can use it to my advantage. Or rather, I can work in accordance to this law.

You wouldn't be reading this book if not for that realization. Before my life transformation, a good chunk of my personal philosophy was the belief that not much depends on my actions. I was afraid that my efforts to get more out of life would be in vain. I would work my ass off just to get exhausted. My dreams couldn't come true.

But I reminded myself of the instances where I did something consistently and got the results. It wasn't a massive action, but it was focused and stretched over a long period of time. I studied during the whole holiday break one year before finishing high school and was able to pass all the final exams without breaking a sweat. I showed up to every university lecture and received a scholarship. I did one series of pushups every day for a few years and I extended my limits. I was eventually able to do more than 120 consecutive pushups.

This realization has shaken my small world. Something clicked in my head. My personal philosophy shifted into "time plus effort equals results."

I developed tiny disciplines, which I practiced consistently: tracking my expenses, tracking my calorie intake, writing, speed-reading. I observed some results almost immediately. Within a month, I was reading almost 50 percent faster. In seven months, I reached my dream weight. Those rapid results kept me going with the disciplines I couldn't have believed would have ever brought me results. Like making money on my own.

I'm a lifelong employee. I started working during my university studies to support my family. I worked in a factory on a production line. I worked as a warehouse man. I did small IT gigs including websites or movie pre-production. After I completed my studies, I was employed as an IT specialist. I'd had five full-time employers since beginning my career. No one ever complained about the quality of my work. In 2008, the project I was working on was stolen from us by the Belgian part of the company. My team was dissolved, most of the guys were laid off, but they kept me to the very end until they could no longer afford to pay me. I'm far from the picture of an ideal employee, but I'm a good enough worker. I could imagine myself pursuing a corporate career.

But my personal philosophy didn't include an ounce of belief that I could make money on my own. In my teenage years, I was involved in multi-level marketing and it finished fast and hard. I dreamed about millions, but I didn't earn a dime. For me that was proof that I was unable to generate an income on my own. It was set in my mind as firmly as the knowledge that sun rises in the east.

So I didn't believe I could have a writing career. But results in other areas of my life caused me to give the law of errors and disciplines a try in this regard, too. I wrote and wrote. I published my first book, then a second. I wasn't breaking even. I published a third book and refined my marketing a bit. The sales grew a bit. After publishing my fourth book, my royalties reached 2 percent of my 9 to 5 job's salary. I started to earn money. It was chicken feed compared with my payroll, but it was enough to crush my belief that I "absolutely cannot earn a dime on my own." Royalties exceeded the cost of covers, blog hosting, and mailing list software. I was like, "Well, at this rate, I'll be able to support myself on my retirement."

Then I published my fifth book, *Master Your Time in 10 Minutes a Day* and the sky has fallen. It became an Amazon bestseller. I earned half of my yearly salary in February 2014.

This law works. I experienced it firsthand. You don't need to believe it to make it work in your life. You don't need to believe in the law of gravity to be grounded either. I stormed the top 80 percent ranks of bestselling indie authors within less than a year because I purposefully adjusted my actions to the law of errors and disciplines.

So, if the law of gravity is applicable in your case, embrace this truth: the universal law of errors and disciplines is applicable to you too. You are probably "using" it now in the same way you use the law of gravity to function. Where you stand in life right now is the effect of compounded errors in judgment or consistent disciplines you performed in your past.

It is very easy to confirm my claim. Take a pen and paper and do a quick five minute self-analysis session. You may check out both sides of the equation. Choose at least one area you are not satisfied with in your life and one in which you feel confident and successful. Ask yourself, "What am I doing on daily basis to deserve such output? What do I do every day that determines this effect?"

For example if you are overweight or obese, examine your eating habits. If you are fit and proud of your body shape, do the same. There are very rare individual cases where the lack of hormonal equilibrium may be blamed, but usually what you eat regulates your weight. Those who eat fast food or sweets and do it consistently over a long period of time are chubby. Those who enjoy salads and cottage cheese are fit. If you enjoy binge eating four times a week, it's not enough to work out at the gym like crazy for four hours once a week. What you consistently do, even in tiny amounts, determine your results.

That's the choice that now stands in front of you. It's a choice you have to make every day. Do you choose what's easy and comfortable right now? Then the chances are that you will be uneasy and uncomfortable in the future. And you will stay much longer in that unpleasant state than if you chose the uncomfortable way today.

Or you can choose to feel the discomfort today and enjoy the comfort in the future. It's just the way this world of ours operates. It's true with money, with relationships, with getting fit, with everything. You can spend money or save it. You can listen attentively or ignore somebody. You can eat a burger or a carrot. Spending money, ignoring the other person, or eating a burger may look like a good idea right now, but you will have to pay the higher price for that in the future.

There is a mind trick involved in this: you will get a bit more comfortable with the uncomfortable with time and, in contrast, you will enjoy the periods of comfort and complacency even more. I seriously encourage you to take the uncomfortable route. Amend your personal philosophy accordingly.

Knowledge Items:

- *One of the laws of nature is that failure is a few errors in judgment repeated every day. Success is a few simple disciplines practiced every day*
- *You are probably "using" it now in the same way you use the law of gravity to function.*

Action Items:

— *Perform a quick 5-minute self-analysis session as described in this chapter.*

The Law's Implications

"Eighty percent of success is showing up."
— Woody Allen

There are plenty of implications to The Law for your life.

1. You are here for the long term and that's how the universe is pre-programmed.

A person's life is measured in decades, not in minutes. Thus, what really counts in your life as a whole is what you do over decades. This power is far greater than what you do from time to time.

2. Now matters.

The simple actions you perform in this exact moment in time have an enormous effect on your decades. Decades consist of the multitude of such moments. The moments compound into the decades of your life. That's why you need to pay attention to your present. You should strive to make each action and each moment perfect. But it is very hard to be conscious every minute of your life. Here the disciplines and habits are very handy. If you develop good habits through simple disciplines, you can transfer big chunks of the control to your subconscious. It will take care of performing the disciplines and keeping you on track without much effort.

3. You matter.

You can consciously build routines and subroutines in your life. You can always step into your *now* and decide to choose a different path. You can consciously avoid a small error in judgment time after time until it becomes automatic. You can consciously choose to act in accordance with your higher purpose and enforce the right discipline.

What's more, you can always change your life's destination by changing your beliefs, thoughts, and actions right here, right now.

4. Everything matters.

You are not some kind of biological machinery. You can't press a button and fix yourself for good. Human beings have the most complex system of anything we have discovered in the universe. And each part of your being depends on the other. When it comes to our bodies, we instinctively grasp that truth. You need all your body parts to work in unison to function to your maximum capabilities. When something hurts you physically, like a tooth, your whole body suffers. You can function or even thrive without a limb or some redundant internal organ (like a kidney). Nick Vujicic is the best example of this. But we also feel it's wrong. It is possible to live more fully when your body is whole.

It's the same with your mind. There is no area in your life that can be neglected without damaging your whole person. There is no improvement you can make in your life that won't improve you as a whole.

Everything matters.

If you allow yourself to err in the case of the kind of food you eat, soon you'll slip in the realm of relationships, productivity, or confidence. If you transform a single aspect of your life, like getting fit, you will soon transform other areas as well.

It's unavoidable.

I didn't believe I could earn a dime on my own. I felt beyond hopeless when dreaming about making a fortune or even making a living from my own ventures. But my level of doubt was much lower in the case of saving money. I struggled for years to keep a bigger chunk of my income, without spectacular results, but there were at least some results. When I changed my attitude and methods toward saving money and started getting results, my whole attitude towards money shifted a bit and I made an attempt to earn some money. In less than a year, my royalties exceeded $1,000, a magic ceiling in the case of indie authors.

And my transformation began with my weight loss attempt. I wanted to lose weight as part of the frustration I had at not being able to implement fully the Getting Things Done system in my life. I definitely failed at that, but this failed attempt left me with a desire to change something in my life. It was strong enough for me to take action.

Everything affects everything. Small, simple, successful disciplines that you stick with for a long time will point your whole being in the right direction. Each of the small errors in judgment may be your first step down the slippery slope of failure.

5. Everyone matters.

We don't really understand humanity. There is always the one in a billion whose deeds surprise scientists. One thing we do know for sure is that we are social creatures. We are interdependent. We affect each other.

Small errors in judgment or simple disciplines repeated over time in the life of a single person will affect everyone around her. The vast majority of personal development teachers use this as an argument for associating with positive and successful people. I invite you to think about it in terms of your personal responsibility. Your errors in judgment and disciplines will certainly affect those around you. The closer someone is to you, the stronger the influence of your errors and disciplines will be.

Knowledge Items:

- *What really counts in your life as a whole is what you do over decades.*
- *Good habits can transfer the control over your present into your future.*
- *You can always step into your now and decide to choose a different path.*
- *There is no area in your life that can be neglected without damaging your whole person. There is no improvement you can make in your life that won't improve you as a whole.*
- *People are interdependent.*

Develop Good Habits

"The only way to improve yourself is to set achievable goals and develop daily habits that move you towards these outcomes."

— S.J. Scott

I believe that there is a single indicator that can validate if a given person's philosophy is "good" or "bad." It's enough to determine if it's abiding by the law of errors and disciplines or not.

Why is it so important? Well, unless your personal philosophy's goal is to make you a Zen master who always goes with the flow and is content with the whole world every single minute, you need a philosophy that will lead you somewhere. We are created for the life journey. We always strive for something more; we want growth. We draw satisfaction from aiming at distant goals, coming closer to achieving them, and setting other, more challenging ones. And if your philosophy doesn't take into account the law of errors and disciplines, it's not likely to lead you anywhere. Rather, you will run in circles like a headless chicken.

I don't see any other law or theory that explains why most people fail and a minority of them succeed. This one does.

Victor Frankl in his book *Man's Search for Meaning* said that people who found their purpose in life at least had a chance to survive. Those who abandoned hope, didn't. Prisoners in death camps had no influence over their circumstances; they only had power over their minds. Some of them chose to live. Some of them died anyway. But all of those who didn't choose to live, died. The power comes from within; it's not fate. You can face fate with your internal attitude and it will make a difference.

I heard this story in *Cultivating The Unshakable Character* by Jim Rohn. At the end of World War II, an American cruiser "Indianapolis" was sunk by a Japanese submarine. Many who made it through the initial attack had to spend days in the water because there were just a few lifeboats and a great shortage of lifejackets. The effort to stay alive was so overwhelming that many sailors simply gave up. Survivors reported that virtually everyone wanted to give up at least once. But whenever someone wanted to quit, the others would talk to him about the people back home who needed him. Those who survived found a reason to live—others who were dependent on them. But didn't those who drowned also have people who needed them? Of course they did, but they chose to think differently, to forget about them. Your mind literally has the power of life or death.

We are so fond of the idea of quantum leaps, of heroic spurts. Of single events that shape our fate. But the truth is that you choose life or death every moment. Eat a burger or a salad? Watch TV or play with the kids? Browse the Internet or finish this project? Become affronted or grateful for the correction? Each of these tiny decisions adds more life or sucks the life out of you. Single outputs are microscopic. Together they are strong like a force of nature. You can't deflect them in a single moment. You couldn't deflect a tsunami with your bare hands either. But if you construct your personal philosophy appropriately, you will be surfing the tsunami wave. This is how the *"Trickle Down Mindset"* works. By making the decision to change your life and letting your choices build momentum, one act at a time.

Thus, I'll urge you to incorporate only a single "mandatory" component into your philosophy: the emphasis on the simple consistent disciplines. Don't try to fly by flapping your arms. Don't try to dive 100 yards deep by just taking a deep breath and submerging yourself. There are some physical constraints in the universe that cannot be overcome by sheer willpower. You may be the one in seven billion that can stretch them, but it's not likely! You'll probably get hurt if you try. Don't try to create your personal philosophy by ignoring the matter of consistent disciplines and repeated errors in judgment. If you need any hint that what you are building will lead you in the right direction, check if it abides by the law of errors and disciplines. If it doesn't, then you are in trouble.

Why is that humans are so inclined to use that law? It's how our brains work. The main part of the brain is our subconscious. It learns through repetition. It loves predictability, stability. It resists change. Your brain loves to keep you on autopilot. That way it takes the least effort. It spends the least amount of precious energy. Habits are the ideal tool for the brain to save energy. You don't need to think too much. You get the cue and you do the action. No thinking involved.

The word "habit" comes from Old French *abit, habit,* from Latin *habitus* 'condition, appearance,' from *habere* 'have, consist of.' The term originally meant 'dress, attire' and the noun habit meant monks' outfit. The habit was an external sign of a monk's internal constitution, which defined their whole lives. Later, the meaning of this word drifted to denote physical or mental constitution.

A modern medical dictionary defines habit as:

- A settled tendency or usual manner of behavior
- A behavior pattern acquired by frequent repetition or physiological exposure that shows itself in regularity or increased facility of performance
- An acquired mode of behavior that has become nearly or completely involuntary
- Addiction

Habits are automatic or semi-automatic behaviors and that's why your brain is so attached to them. They allow your brain to bypass the conscious mind and preserve the energy. And strangely enough, habits are in line with the law of errors and disciplines.

You may have formed a habit of smiling as soon as you see your spouse. Now, each time you see him or her, you smile. That's a positive habit. But you can also turn some disciplines into a habit. Small and simple things like flossing your teeth or doing a consecutive series of pushups every morning. A single instance of such behavior means almost nothing. Repeated over time it provides some advantages. Repeated consistently, it becomes a habit, which conserves your willpower and energy resources. It is supervised via the minimal investment of attention and it automatically yields profits.

A vice is the reverse of a habit.

Habits work for you, vices work against you. You may fall into the trap of consistently repeating small errors, like enjoying a chocolate bar after a meal. This repetition becomes your habit; in this case even an addiction. A small error becomes the automatic behavior bypassing your consciousness. After a while, because sugar is a powerful narcotic, reaching out for a bar of chocolate after a meal is a part of your constitution; it's in some strange way part of *you*.

After a couple of years, you wake up and notice that you are 40 pounds heavier. A small error repeated over time caused it. The law of errors materialized.

You are what you consistently do. And your consistent action derives from your frame of thoughts, from your personal philosophy. The right philosophy employs the law of errors and disciplines to your advantage. It also prevents you from making the small errors in judgment and the effects of addiction.

The most effective form of fighting addiction is prevention. If you don't develop an addiction, you won't be forced to spend an incredible amount of energy, willpower, time, and resources on eliminating it. Instead, you'll direct your energy into achieving your goals and tasks at hand.

For example, I'm guilty of compulsive stats and email checking. I do it involuntarily. Whenever I have a couple of minutes online to spare, my mouse cursor goes to the icon of my email program. It's a time-wasting addiction. But I didn't come up with a smart plan to overcome my addiction. I refused to focus my attention on it. I focus on my simple disciplines instead. I have plenty of them. This leaves me very little leeway for things like spending hours on mindless surfing on the Internet. Some of my disciplines are quite big, like writing 1000 words a day. This is my high-priority task. I focus on it every morning and it doesn't leave much space for addictions.

The right philosophy simply starves your addictions and vices by transferring your attention to other areas.

I ramble about The Law of Errors and Disciplines because it's so crucial. You can't ignore it. You can't say you don't believe it works. You can say the same about the law of gravity, but it won't change the fact that you are grounded to the Earth. You can choose to "ignore" the law of gravity and jump off a cliff because you want to soar. But the law of gravity won't ignore you and you will be crushed on the rocks below.

Going further with the analogy, you can jump off the cliff by paragliding and enjoy a nice flight. But sooner or later, you will have to land. Not even birds can fly their whole life.

You can use some tools and tricks to accelerate your growth without discipline or to postpone the effects of small errors in judgment for some time. But you can't change the basic law of the universe. You will "land" sooner or later and it may be a painful experience.

I strongly encourage you to adapt your philosophy to this Law. Always take it into account, because it surely won't ignore you. There are shortcuts to success, no doubt about it. You can see those rare rags-to-riches stories in the media all the time. Every week there are also new stories of lottery winners. Both kinds of stories are hard to replicate.

Don't count on luck or a rapid breakthrough. Create your own luck or breakthrough by sticking with your simple disciplines for a long time.

Start thinking in terms of simple daily disciplines that can positively affect you and those around you. It's a surefire way to create lasting change in your life. When it's small and simple, your brain doesn't resist the action. It judges it as something "easy to do," and rightly so. When this action is repeated many times over, your brain learns to accept and embrace it. With time, the discipline will become an inseparable part of your constitution. And, most important, it will drive your results, because that's the law of the universe.

Knowledge Items:

— *Create your own luck or breakthrough by sticking with your simple disciplines for a long time.*
— *Your brain doesn't resist action if it's small and simple.*

The Ten-Minute Philosophy

"The future is something which everyone reaches at the rate of 60 minutes an hour, whatever he does, whoever he is."

— C.S. Lewis

I called my personal philosophy The Ten-Minute Philosophy, because it's built around ten-minute activities. It's based on *The Slight Edge* philosophy, but modified to my personal needs and circumstances. It was not fully formed initially. I just tried different things and kept what was working. It was the trial and error process.

When I read *The Slight Edge* in August 2012, I decided to give the philosophy presented there a try. I had quite a lot of time to spare. I started new habits, six of which were ten minutes long. Others varied in terms of time investment, but at the beginning, the longest—listening to podcasts and motivational materials— was only fifteen minutes maximum.

Once I gave this new attitude and these new habits a chance, my life changed rapidly. And at the core of my transformation were those ten-minute activities, which I considered easy to do (or to not do). It was amazing how such tiny actions repeated over time revolutionized my whole life.

While developing my new habits, I was determined to stick with them for a minimum of 30 days. However, in the case of studying the Bible, I was determined to form a lifelong habit.

The basis of my determination was my frustration. I wasn't satisfied with how my life had turned out so far. My recent philosophy hadn't brought me much closer to the things and qualities I desired. I needed something new. My past experiences convinced me that there was a lot of merit in *The*

Slight Edge philosophy. And at the basis of this philosophy lies the law of errors and disciplines.

So the core assumption of my new philosophy was this Law. The longer I adhered to it, the better results I observed, up to the point where I was fully convinced it was true and universal. Then I committed to it even more. I built a multitude of disciplines, just for the fun of it. And there were always some results.

Developing my new personal philosophy, I didn't mimic big gurus and their systems of belief. Firstly, I'm highly skeptical about anyone who claims to want only good things for me and then asks for money to help me. Also, my culture does not worship success the way Western culture does. We received our unfair share of communist indoctrination about blood-lusting capitalists and then the transformation of my country, which I'm sad to say, confirmed a lot of these stereotypes. Lots of people with no remorse abused the system, abused their employees and clients, and made fortunes. We experienced in Poland over a period of fifteen years the kind of wild capitalism that prevailed in America throughout the nineteenth century.

But an even greater factor was that I very quickly realized that the advice of millionaires applies best to millionaires. Most of those people live in ivory towers. They enjoy levels of freedom that are unattainable for most people. They share solid advice worth millions of dollars, but they aren't applicable to the 9-to-5 worker.

I was (and still am) a slave of my past choices. I have a mortgage that will be paid off over the next 35 years. I have a wife and three kids. I cannot abandon everything and start a full-time writing career from scratch. Writing is my passion. I knew that as soon as I examined my soul for the first time in fifteen years. I'm amazed each time someone praises my style and it has happened more times that I can count in this past year. But I had exactly *zero* experience when I started publishing at the age of 34. It took me eight months to earn serious money. And throughout this time, my past obligations were holding me to my old life. Job. Bills. Mortgage. Family. Lifelong addictions. Poor physical shape. Poor spiritual growth. I needed to untangle the web of past obligations before I could apply millionaires' advice in the wider spectrum. I needed to fix my relationship with God, finances, body, professional position, and bad habits all at once. I was not in a position to pick pieces of gurus' advice that were most effective. I picked those that could be applied immediately in my life.

And a "personal" component in this concept means that your philosophy is individual, unique, one-time, just-for-you. You can't simply take someone else's ideas and use them effectively. You must own them in order to have them work for you. I took ownership of the concept of small errors in judgment and consistent disciplines by examining my past experiences. I discovered several instances successes and failures and realized I could credit them to the small errors in judgment or simple consistent disciplines accordingly. I found The Law actually worked in my life before I even knew the concept. I desired change, so I absorbed this Law as a part of my perspective, albeit temporarily.

Then I started to expand my philosophy. I was going through a vast amount of personal development materials— audio, videos, and books. I had a contact within the personal development industry in my teens, but I only scratched the surface then. I didn't just blindly accept everything I read, heard, or saw. I absorbed only those elements of new teachings I could easily adapt to my current lifestyle. For example I had (and still have) a thing called a job with a four-hour commute, something that no millionaire I know has to put up with. I'm in relationships with people whom I could easily have labeled "negative," starting with my wife and finishing with my workmates. But I refused to label them. I needed to work out my own methods of dealing with them. The standard advice— "ditch the losers"—was hardly applicable because according to millionaire's standards, everyone around me is a loser.

I took the ideas, tried them, and gradually incorporated those that I found helpful. That's the way I recommend you develop your philosophy, too. It's the only sensible way. You can only do what you believe is true. If you don't believe that the universe is constructed of energy and that the human brain is a system receiving and sending vibrations through the universe's layers of energy, you won't focus on your vision consistently enough or strongly enough. For every effort you consciously put into making this Law of Attraction happen, you will use twice as much subconscious effort to sabotage it.

I practiced new ideas almost always in "probation mood" and almost always, they became permanent. I was trying new things and looking for confirmation that they worked. I read about paying yourself first in David Bach's book and stashed away 2.8 percent of my income. It went against my gut feelings and lifelong indoctrination, but I did it anyway. Within a few months, I saw that it was really working, that my savings were growing. I read in *The Compound Effect* by Warren Hardy about a gratitude journal he wrote about his wife. In *The Slight Edge* online community, I met a guy who did the same. I started the gratitude journal about my wife with one entry a day. It took me less than six months to recognize the soothing effect gratitude has on my whole being, and I expanded it to my kids and then to my whole life. Nowadays I write down no fewer than 25 entries in my three different gratitude journals.

Action Items:

- *Practice new ideas in "probation mood"*
- *Take the ideas, try them, and gradually incorporate those that you find helpful.*
- *While developing new habits, resolve to stick with them for a minimum of 30 days.*

Three-Dimensional Philosophy

"A human being always acts and feels and performs in accordance with what he imagines to be true about himself and his environment."

— Maxwell Maltz

Personal philosophy is a system for conduct of life. It consists of thoughts, experiences, interpretation attached to those experiences, relationships, emotions, data, data interpretations, and a myriad of other things. Life is complicated and complex; so is a system for conducting it. So in order to make it more bearable, easier to comprehend, and manageable, I will describe this concept in a way the human brain loves to act: with generalization and simplification.

I recognize three main elements shaping personal philosophy: people, data input sources, and your individual interpretation of data. Because everything matters and everything affects everything else, it's enough to focus on these three elements and develop a successful personal philosophy.

As previously explained, if your personal philosophy doesn't bring you closer to the outputs you really desire, it is stale. All you need is to refresh it a bit and keep changing it in the right direction. It's enough to get involved with new people, to alter a bit the sources of your data input, and attach a new interpretation to the data you receive. It will transform your personal philosophy and transform your life.

People may be regarded as data input sources too. But there is something distinct in humanity. It is stronger to hear the information from another man than to read the same information in a book. Relationships and interactions stir more emotions and thoughts than any other way of receiving information. People have a profound influence on your philosophy. People are special and cannot be treated like a radio show or a book. I'll expose how it works by sticking with the example of the process of reforming my philosophy in 2012.

I met new people. A month after reading *The Slight Edge*, I joined its online community. It is now sadly neglected, but it was quite alive when I signed up. As you know, the idea of my gratitude journal was partly born out of reading about the experiences of a member of *The Slight Edge* community. It is just a single instance showing how meeting new people may affect your worldview.

However, interaction in that community was an experience very similar to those I had in the past with online forums. I was involved in communities gathered around my hobbies: computers and card games. It is a nice feeling to meet like-minded people and exchange experiences. Nice, that's all.

At the beginning of 2013, I joined another online community and it was a transcending experience. I took part in the Transformation Contest organized by Early to Rise. There were about 40,000 participants from all over the world. We spent three months together in the deeply committed online community. I met new friends there. We shared our life stories; we hid nothing. Deep stuff like life and death, like losing someone or falling in love. Those people know some things about me that even my family doesn't.

Within a month, this event transformed from a simple contest to an encouragement volcano. We cheered up and encouraged each other. We prayed for each other. We offered comfort to each other. It was an empowering experience. It fostered an amazing level of trust between the participants. I met half a dozen friends there from all over the world. "Friends" in a Polish meaning of the word—people who I am ready to die for. I met a lot more acquaintances. To this day, we hang out together and we are ready to do a favor for any member of the Transformation Contest.

Just two concrete instances of how much this experience altered my life.

1. On Feb. 26, 2013, I shared on my Transformation Contest wall my personal mission statement creation process. One of my friends commented: *"You should write an e-book about this."* I took her advice seriously and *A Personal Mission Statement: Your Roadmap to Happiness* was my first work ever published. It has sold 410 copies in the last 90 days.

2. English is not my native language and when I was starting my writing career, it was much worse than today. I needed a native proofreader but I had no funds to pay for the service and no idea how to get one. I posted the first draft of my book on the Transformation Challenge Facebook group. Diane Arms was impressed with my openness and she volunteered to edit my book. She did it with my first four works. Without her help, I could never have moved forward with my publishing venture.

The second cornerstone of personal philosophy is data input sources. Inspired by Jeff Olson's advice to read ten pages of a good book every day, I introduced some changes to what information, how, and in what amounts I consumed. I had a habit of doing a Weider (exercise) series for fifteen minutes each morning. So I started to listen to audio materials. I also completely changed the type of books I was reading. I replaced pulp fiction books with philosophy, personal development, spiritual, and business books. One of the first six habits I started at the beginning of my transformation was reading a book written by a saint for ten minutes a day. You can check out my Goodreads profile to observe this transition in my lectures in the past two years.

Exposing myself to new kinds of information bore fruit within a couple of months. A few examples:

- I read *The 7 Habits of Highly Effective People* and created my personal mission statement
- I read *The Compound Effect* and started my first gratitude journal.
- I read *Start Over, Finish Rich* by David Bach and was convinced I had to pay myself first, which translated into about $7000 in savings in 18 months.

The last element—interpretation of emotions, experiences and data—is the least tangible of the cornerstones, but important nonetheless. Your internal voice is extremely significant in the process of absorbing new ideas. I could read Mr. Bach's advice and comment on it internally—*"What BS! I know everything about savings. I've been tracking the exact amounts on my savings account for the last three years. Paying myself first? What a stupid idea! And what will I eat, when the funds run dry in the middle of the month?"* Instead, I said, *"It's counterintuitive, but this guy is a millionaire and I'm not. Let's try it and see how this works."*

You may move to a different state or country, you may change your social environment altogether, you may read new books and listen to new coaches, but if you don't alter your self-talk a bit, it will all be in vain. You will disregard new information and advice and sooner or later, you will go back to your old ways.

Knowledge Items:

- *It's enough to focus on three pillars to develop a successful personal philosophy: data sources, people, and internal interpretation.*

Time for an Upgrade

"Anyone who wants to sell you overnight success or wealth is not interested in your success; they are interested in your money."

— Bo Bennett

I hope I drove the point home and you embraced the idea that the way your mind functions dictates the outcomes in your life.

Can you connect the dots? Do you see how specific types of mindsets generate specific results in your life? If they are not satisfying, it's time to transform your philosophy. The important thing here is not to dwell on what's unsatisfactory in your life, not to beat yourself up for it, but to objectively observe your conditions and the trends.

If you progress in specific areas, then the chances are your philosophy is not so rotten after all. The lack of satisfaction comes from impatience or your high expectations, which usually are a result of comparing yourself to others.

Let's say you are obese. You are 5 feet 5 inches and weigh 200 pounds. But a year ago, you weighed 240 pounds. You *are* doing something right. Your mindset is not all trash.

Or you have $5 million in your savings account and don't need to work if you don't want to. That's great. Ninety-eight percent of the population would like to be in your place. However, two years ago you inherited $25 million. Hey, there is something wrong with your attitude toward money.

Okay, you know you need a better philosophy, so how do you change it? Should you try to revolutionize it and develop it from scratch or rather painfully discard one rotten element after another and replace them with a more healthy construction?

I'm almost sure your intuition suggests you go on a rampage. Ditch the old, ineffective methods! Do as many things as possible as fast as possible! Your old philosophy has already cost you a lot of priceless time, which may never be reclaimed. All of that is fine and true, but you are not a *tabula rasa*.

Your intuition is partly right. It is possible to entirely rebuild your personal philosophy. People do it all the time. Mark Bowness transformed his life at the age of 26. A single event — his own failed suicide attempt—made him examine all his previous beliefs and change them practically within one day. You can radically change all three elements that comprise personal philosophy. You can change who you interact with in a single moment. You can move to a different town, state, country, or continent. You can change your data digesting habits: throw away the TV, destroy your mobile phone, install a firewall app on your computer and block all the news sites. Or you can start saying to yourself whenever you encounter an unfortunate event that "every obstacle is a chance if viewed as an opportunity for growth or self-mastery."

However, you need to realize that such drastic measures also have a drastic cost attached to them. For example, I hate TV as it is today, but I dread to think how my wife would react if I threw the set out the window. I wouldn't have to watch it for some time, but the price would be horrendous.

Building an entirely new philosophy is like joining a religious order. You abandon your old life. You change the whole social fabric of your life; you surround yourself with totally new people. You change the sources of information. Worldly sources become secondary at best. You focus on the holy teachings and the teachings of holiness.

If your calling is the real deal, you will also change your internal dialog, the interpretation of events and actions you encounter and/ or perform. You and your life will change completely within a short period of time.

But they are not so eager to accept a fresh convert into religious orders. They know that the resolution may be temporary. That the freshman may slip back into his old ways after several months and find himself unfit for the new way of life. That's why practically every respected religious order introduces the institution of novitiate. They accept a candidate for a set period, usually for a year or longer to see if he can persevere. During that time, he is also examining himself, to see if he really finds this new life compelling.

There are genuine converts who are able to transform their lives within a few days, but they are rare birds. And they come into an order the same way ordinary mortals do—through the probation period. Religious orders accumulated their wisdom over thousands of years. Use their balanced approach to prepare your own life revolution. Break yourself in gradually.

Besides, I can't teach you how to develop an entirely new personal philosophy from scratch, because I didn't do it. I meticulously transformed my old philosophy, and I advise you to do the same.

Sudden transformations are uncommon. You hear about them a lot because they are so spectacular and the media loves them. But for every sudden breakthrough, there are 999 more mundane and slower but equally effective stories of development.

And usually you can find some background preparations that took years to develop before the revolution occurred. Saint Paul converted to Christianity in a single encounter. But he was prepared. He was a very educated Jew. He knew all the old scriptures. He was also introduced to Christianity by the believers he persecuted. He needed just a "gentle" push to convert. His story couldn't materialize in some pagan who didn't even realize that there was one God. He was carefully prepared for years to reach this single moment of catharsis.

Saint Augustin was a lecher and flibbertigibbet. He enjoyed a worldly life to its fullest. But he was also the son of a very pious woman and was exposed to her lessons in his early years. She also prayed for him for all the years he pursued the pleasures of flesh.

So, yes, their transformations were unexpected. What sane person would believe that a murderer or lecher could transform so quickly into a saint? But in hindsight, it's clear that it didn't happen out of the blue. Their new philosophy was founded on their past experiences and knowledge. And this is the way you should seek your transformation, your shift in your personal philosophy.

Your current personal philosophy could be messy and probably is. You are not in the place you desire in life. You want a better body, health, higher bank balance, finer things, better relationships, better education. You didn't get them because of your mindset. However, your mindset contains a lot of gems, a lot of solid parts upon which you can build your new life. Everything that has happened in your life to date has prepared you for your upgraded philosophy.

And there is one additional advantage in admitting that your previous philosophy led you to your current results—you take responsibility for your past decisions, actions, and results. It's irrational, but empowering. It's irrational because you can't take responsibility for the earthquake that destroyed your house. But it's empowering because you feel you are in control of your life. It was you who decided to settle in that spot where there was a risk of earthquakes. Your decision led you to your current pitiful situation, so your decision can also bring you out of it. That's the attitude shared by many successful people, and it's worth adopting.

Knowledge Items:

- *Don't revolutionize your philosophy; drastic measures also have a drastic cost attached to them.*

Action Items:

- *Admit that your previous philosophy led you to your current results. Repeat the self-analysis exercise from the chapter, The Law of Nature.*

Changing Course

"You cannot change your destination overnight,
but you can change your direction overnight."

— Jim Rohn

In the previous chapter, we concluded that you are at this point in your life because your beliefs, thoughts, and actions led you to this exact point. And it's not a bright point or you wouldn't be looking for ways to improve your life.

So, are you a complete failure? Your negative self-talk may tend to agree with that not-so-gently put question, but I am sure you are not.

First of all, you are alive. It means that you have already gathered years of experience and winning experience at that. There are some of your peers who didn't make it. You did. That's no small feat.

Secondly, you are reading this book. It says a lot about you. Obviously you can read. You also want to improve your life. That means you have a high enough level of integrity to realize that you are not perfect. You are able to admit mistakes. You are humble and willing to learn. You have stuck with me so far, enduring my frequent religious references, so you are religious yourself or open minded and tolerant.

I could go on with the list of your positive traits for a few more paragraphs, but I think you get the point. You are not a complete failure, whatever your external circumstances are. Your current personal philosophy is a mishmash of right and wrong beliefs and habits. You can build on what you have. And you shouldn't rush this redevelopment.

Yes, it would be nice to have a new shiny personal philosophy tomorrow that would skyrocket you to the ranks of millionaires in a few months. But it is unreasonable to expect it to happen. Forget about instant gratification. Forget about quantum leaps. Consider those terms as the products of an alien civilization. Absolutely foreign and incomprehensible.

You are a human being and rapid transformation is not a trait you are equipped with. Your brain doesn't work that way. If it meets with a rapid change, it reacts with instant resistance. But when you introduce changes slowly and gradually, your subconscious won't even recognize them as changes. It will sublimate them and after some time it will defend those new ideas as its own. Gratification and quantum leaps will come. But they will be the fruits of a long, consistent effort. That's how they *always* materialize.

The bad news is that you just can't change your life in a single moment. The good news is that you can instantly change your life's *direction*. Once you decide to adjust, to incorporate one idea or concept into your mind, the overall direction of your life will drastically change. And the longer you stick with this adjustment, the more drastic change will materialize. Think of a plane starting in New York and heading to Los Angeles. A tiny change of course of only one degree will change its destination by 40 miles. Just three degrees south or north is the difference between San Diego and Bakersfield. That's the gap between errors in judgment and disciplines.

Another thing I want you to contemplate when you are beginning to reconstruct your personal philosophy is your life span. How long will you live? Well, you don't know. You can hope at most to live a certain number of years. But no matter if you are a teenager or a venerable sage, no matter if you will die in an accident, of sickness, or old age, one thing is sure: you will live as long as it takes.

And guess how long your personal philosophy will serve you? Yep. Until the end of your life. In my opinion, as a believer, it will serve you much longer than that. It will serve you into infinity.

You may not believe that and that's fine. Forget the afterlife. The impact of your personal philosophy will continue beyond your lifespan. Even if you are reduced to a heap of proteins, your past choices will affect others. For example, if saving money was part of your philosophy, you will leave an inheritance for your relatives and/or charities of your choice. If creation was a part of your philosophy, you will leave a legacy of paintings or musical works or writings. If Jim Rohn hadn't changed his personal philosophy, he wouldn't have left numerous audio programs and books for others to develop themselves. I would have been a different person without that and you probably wouldn't be reading this book right now.

So it's good to emphasize the long-term perspective in your philosophy. Don't worry about naysayers who claim that it will keep you from achieving your short-term goals. If that's the case, then those goals were not worth achieving. Just focus on your daily job and lifelong vision and you will exceed your goals. Before publishing *Master Your Time*, I would have been stoked if I'd earned 5 percent of my salary but I had *no* immediate goals connected to it. I was only focused on creating the best possible book for busy people interested in increasing their productivity. And a new book was just a small puzzle in the big picture of my life. I was taken completely by surprise when that book became a bestseller. Since then the lowest level my royalties have reached have been 16 percent of my salary.

There is magic in long-term thinking, the one utilizing the law of errors and disciplines. The long-term perspective is fruitful even within a short time span, but the opposite is not true. Chasing medium-sized goals one after another without thinking about the long-term consequences is likely to lead to emptiness.

Knowledge Items:

- *You are not a complete failure.*
- *It is unreasonable to develop a new shiny personal philosophy tomorrow.*
- *The long-term perspective is fruitful even within a short time span; the opposite is not true.*

Analyze Your Data Sources

"Garbage in, garbage out."

— Anonymous

I encourage you to first address your data sources. Change the media from which you obtain information. Change the amount of time you employ to get information. I don't mean you should turn off your TV for good because you enjoy watching 30 minutes of the evening news every day. Don't focus on what's wrong with the current way you gather data. It's helpful if you target the most destructive data inputs responsible for your worldview, but it's not necessary to develop an improved personal philosophy.

All you need is to introduce positive changes and focus on them. New beliefs and ideas will challenge your current philosophy and habits. With time, you will realize what was wrong. And you won't have to struggle to give up on those not-so-supportive input sources. You will want to dedicate more time to your new and effective ways of conducting your life. The old customs will naturally die out.

To stick with those changes, develop new habits. It's essential to adopt new habits of ingesting information. You need automatic routines to take care of this element of reshaping your philosophy. Changing your social environment and the interpretation of your experiences is much harder than changing your data sources. You need more conscious effort to master them. That's why you should employ habits in those cases, too. Don't stop at changing what you read or listen to. Develop new habits that will help you meet new people. Make a habit of examining your speech patterns, your self-talk, and your thoughts.

Everything is easier when you use automatic routines. A common theme across the whole personal development realm is to use the power of habits to your advantage. This advice is not a recommendation of theoreticians. It was tested in practice time after time. Successful people almost unanimously recommend the use of habits as the most formidable tool for reaching one's goals. Jim Rohn, Leo Babauta, Jeff Olson, Stephen R. Covey, John D. Rockefeller, Thomas Edison—all of them were employing habits in their pursuits.

Your brain was designed to utilize habits. They just work. It's not willpower. It's not the purpose, drive, or vision. It's not the attractiveness of new activities. Habits are the most effective tools of transformation. Use this aspect of your brain to maximize the transformation and ease the effort of introducing the change.

The best way to develop new habits is to build them on the old ones. When I decided to transform my life, I had a habit of doing a Weider series in the morning for fifteen minutes. It never occurred to me that I could utilize this time. One of the first new habits I adopted was listening to audio programs during this exercise. It opened my mind to a variety of ideas. Over a period of almost two years, I listened to a few audio books, several audio programs, and hundreds of podcasts. My most profound experience involved with this discipline was learning a variant of Muscle Testing Techniques, which I used the very same day in practice. It was my first milestone to overcoming my shyness. It led me to writing my book *From Shy to Hi*. I did nothing more than commit to listening to audio for fifteen minutes a day and it changed my life and the lives of others.

All the leaders are readers. I heard this slogan numerous times and felt good about myself because I'm an avid reader. I read in Norton Beau's *Extreme Confidence* that he has been studying the lives of successful people for over three years, and he has not came across *a single* extremely successful person who *did not* read books.

I can't preach reading books strongly enough. Ditch all the excuses! Just do it. If you read at least ten pages of a good book every day, it will translate to eight to ten books read within one year. If it seems daunting because you don't like to read, start with a couple of pages a day. The worst thing you can do is to ignore this advice and not read at all.

You are lucky to live in the Internet era. There are a multitude of blogs on every subject imaginable. You can learn about parenting, healthy eating, starting a new business, becoming an author, and a thousand other things. Carefully select two or three blogs in an interesting area and follow them very closely. I recommend you avoid "gurus"—popular blogs with gigantic followings. Find someone closer to your level, who has had some success but still has time and a desire to interact with his audience. This kind of interaction on the Internet touches on another pillar of rebuilding your personal philosophy: meeting new people. Not only does the blog owner count, but also his followers. The comments section is a great place to meet new acquaintances. You get two advantages with one stroke. You can also automate your blog readings by using RSS feeds.

I strongly dislike learning from videos, but you may prefer this. And there are a lot of valuable video materials on the Internet. As with blogs, there are a multitude of specialized channels on YouTube. To expand your horizons, I recommend TED talks. If you prefer to consume content offline (as I do), there are free tools that allow you to download videos from most of the sites, including YouTube. I recommend Flash Video Downloader if you use Firefox or HD Transform.

Audio is another way to get new ideas and knowledge. You can utilize a lot of opportunities to listen to audio materials: doing household chores, exercising, commuting, driving, going shopping. The list is endless. You can subscribe to your favorite podcasts and download them automatically into your device.

You can even find some valuable TV programs to follow. It's hard for me to imagine, but there are *some* such programs. Skip the trash. I don't have time to go through garbage, that's why I don't turn on the TV at all. I can find all I need to learn on the Internet and consume the content in the way I want, at the time I prefer.

With such a variety of data sources, you can surely find something that will work *for you*. Nowadays we are more threatened with information overload than with data scarcity. So carefully choose a couple of new inputs and develop new habits of plugging into them. Some useful ideas:

- Read ten pages of a good book a day
- Listen to one podcast episode a day
- Watch one TED talk a day
- Read a single specialized blog post a day
- Listen to educational/motivational audio materials for fifteen minutes a day
- Read a single random blog post a day (just type an interesting topic into Google)

Approach these activities like any other serious habit-building activity. Design the process. Try to connect your new habits with existing ones, like I did with my exercises. Find your cue, a trigger for starting an activity, like leaving a book on your bedside table, so every time you lie down, you read ten pages of it. Set alarms or reminders. Track a new habit. Make it a point to do both the habit itself and track it every day.

Action Items:

- *Develop at least one single new data-absorbing habit.*
- *Connect your new habits with existing ones; find your cue*
- *Track a new habit.*

Analyze Yourself

"He who knows others is wise; he who knows himself is enlightened."

— Lao Tzu

Begin from within yourself. You know yourself in the most intimate ways. You are a mine of information about you. Sadly, most of us never try to touch this repository of self-knowledge. Ever.

I was able to avoid self-analysis for almost sixteen years. A few very serious conversations with close friends or family members, a yearly retreat with my church community where I was given obligatory spiritual exercises —that was all.

If you feel resistance against self-analysis, you can probably relate to my feelings from that period. I didn't want to look deep inside myself because I generally despised myself. Only a thin layer of good intentions and good deeds was worthy of praise. Under it was a deep reservoir of laziness, complacency, and middle-class comfort. On the other hand, when I started serious analysis after my transformation, I was terrified of an eventual greatness in me. Both things— below the surface of my life and above it—were uncomfortable to contemplate, so I tried very hard to not think about them at all.

However, you can speed up the process of upgrading your personal philosophy by getting to know yourself.

It makes perfect sense. Of course, you can organize some kind of retreat, sit with a list of life and death questions, meditate upon them, ponder them, and resolve them from within, let's say, within three days. But have you three days to spare? You are busy living! Besides, you are not static. New questions will appear in your life sooner or later. The old answers will slightly evolve. A simple daily discipline is a better solution for facing life's challenges. And one more thing. If you drain yourself answering all the important questions, you may be overwhelmed by the answers. You will suddenly realize how much work is awaiting you and how much effort you need to put into straightening out contorted parts of your life.

Self-examination is part of a personal philosophy for many successful people. Socrates, the Greek philosopher who invented the term "philosophy" had a motto: "Know thyself." Many successful people recommended journaling as a way to keep in touch with yourself and to adjust your personal philosophy. Among famous diarists were Lewis Carrol, the author of *Alice's Adventures in Wonderland*; Virginia Woolf, an English novelist; British Prime Minister Winston Churchill; and many American presidents including George Washington, John Quincy Adams, Thomas Jefferson, Ronald Reagan, and Harry S. Truman.

Keeping a daily journal is a great discipline for constantly maintaining a high level of self-knowledge. It will reveal the truth about you piece by piece. You will rebuild yourself one bit at a time. The revolution may be stretched out, but it will become a lasting one, and it won't be any less impressive than the one done within three days.

If I were you, I would consider keeping a journal as your main indicator of how serious you are about this whole "adjusting personal philosophy" thing. It's a simple activity. Everybody can keep a journal. With the level of technology we have achieved, you can be even limbless and keep an audio or video journal. But the vast majority of our society has two strong hands, good eyesight, and has mastered the skill of writing (or typing), yet still doesn't keep a journal. Not doing so is an error in judgment repeated over time. And absolutely any kind of journal qualifies. Even a food journal can be a valuable source of self-information. Keep a food journal for a couple of months and you will recognize patterns. Are you consistent?

Are your cheat days devolving into cheat weeks? Are you better at abstaining from your favorite (and caloric) foods or at introducing a new type of healthy food? Do you prefer regularity or novelty? Many people track their moods in their food journals or note down the time and duration of every meal. All this data can be translated into your character's traits.

How you structure your journal is entirely up to you. It may be a very focused kind of journal, such as a food, time, or a gratitude journal. Or you may ramble for five minutes each evening about your emotions like a teenager. Techniques can be freestyle too: Video, audio, or online blogs or just good old school notepads and pens work. There is only one iron clad rule when it comes to doing it right: do it consistently.

Before my transformation, I had never kept any kind of journal longer than a couple of months and the last time I did so was when I was a teenager. Now I keep six of them:

1. My daily Bible study, where I write just a few sentences about the specific fragment I found speaking to me that day;
2. Gratitude journal about my wife, where I write at least one thing I'm grateful for or about her.
3. Gratitude journal for my kids, where I write at least three entries about each of my three kids.
4. General purpose gratitude journal, where I write about 10 to 20 things I'm grateful for this very day. I include also my daily achievements in that journal; I'm grateful for them too.
5. My progress journal, where I write everything I did for my business that day and, from time to time, some ruminations.
6. My self-analysis journal.

I didn't start them all at once. It was a gradual process that took me about nine months.

I encourage you to start by tracking your data sources. Carry a pocket notepad with you at all times for one week and jot down what you read, listen to, watch, and with whom you speak and meet. You can extend the scope of this discipline: note the time each of these took you, track if you label this input as positive or negative, the conversation subjects (small talk, job, spirituality), and whatever else comes to mind.

Start journaling today. Only you can reveal the treasures that are hidden inside you.

If you want to take massive action from the start, when your motivation is at its peak, do some hefty self-examination sessions. I can't replace you in this task, but I can provide you with some support. I give you questions and exercises. Answer them all at once or one by one, in one or ten sessions, in this particular order or one that is more suitable for you. You are in charge of this mission. It's up to you.

What activities are you trying to avoid? Why?

What do you consider your greatest failure? Why?

What do you consider your greatest success? Why? Was it hard to choose this one? Can you think of more success examples?

What are you good at? Why?

What have you always wanted to do but have been afraid to attempt?

List your life's goals. Imagine you have no limitations, that success is guaranteed. Which one goal would you choose to achieve? Why this one?

Imagine that you have only six months left to live. How would it change your actions?

Recall the time when you felt most loved. Why did you feel loved then?

Visualize how your life will be in 5, 10, and 20 years from now if you don't make any significant decisions during these years. Imagine letting your life "go with the flow." Dwell on your finances, health, relationships, personal growth, spirituality, career. Do you really want your life to look like this? What is missing in these pictures? Think more in terms of values and feelings than of physical possessions.

Visualize your own funeral. Who is there? What are your family, friends, church members, and work mates saying about you? Write your own specific eulogy. Actually write it out.

Don't stop at these tasks. Seriously consider forming a self-analysis habit. Once you start, you will find it easy to continue. Each morning I sit down with a pen in my hand and for about ten minutes, I write about myself: my goals, problems, plans, obstacles, dreams, achievements, struggles, relationships, etc. At the beginning, I was afraid I would quickly exhaust the topics but a year later, I still have a fresh subject to ponder. Human nature is amazingly complex. You will find something worth thinking about every time, I assure you.

I usually ask myself a question and try to answer it comprehensively. For example, how would you like your life to be in ten years? If I find the subject too ample, I continue answering the question for the next day.

Here is good material for such an exercise. Examine your attitude toward the advice I have already written about: the law of errors and disciplines,, long-term perspective, personal responsibility for your life's outputs, the importance of self-analysis. Ask yourself, "Do I believe this is true? Why? Why not; then what's true in this regard? Which of my experiences support my point of view?"

I'll continue to emphasize this point. It's *your* personal philosophy. You own it. You must embrace those "right" pieces as your own. Maybe they are not right for you, maybe you have been diagnosed with end-stage cancer and long-term perspectives are not valid for you. I don't know, but you know yourself and your situation. Use that knowledge.

One of the almost universal pieces of successful people's philosophies is "stop hanging out with negative people." For me it was not acceptable. Tell me how the "negative" people are supposed to change if they have no example to follow? From where should they get inspiration to transform? Severing my relationships with them was in my eyes like abandoning them. I embraced two other bits of philosophy.

First, that I'm solely responsible for my reactions. No one can "drag me down" if I don't allow it first in my mind. I didn't consciously break any relationships. I changed the things I was focusing on. I almost stopped playing the computer games and my favorite card game. My playing buddies see me *a lot* less often.

Second, that I must be the change I want to see in others. I don't dwell on their "negativity." I don't mull over how they behaved unjustly towards me or how their philosophy and deeds are wrong, debilitating, and not constructive. That's their life and they can do whatever they wish with it. I focus on being the best "me" I can be.

Maybe I could progress faster without them. Quite possibly. A million millionaires are preaching this rule of ditching the disturbers, so it must have some merit. But I still progress nonetheless and I feel much more "me" doing it my way.

Another idea for self-examination is creating and using your personal mission statement. It's your personal constitution, which "focuses on what you want to be (character) and to do (contributions and achievements) and on the values or principles upon which being and doing are based."[1] Composing your own mission statement is a self-examination experience in itself, but it's just the beginning. Once you have it, you refer to it every day; you read it, listen to it, repeat it in your mind. It's enough to know those words by heart to examine every information input through them. You almost automatically correct your actions to be in accordance with your mission.

A personal mission statement is a very effective tool for transformation. I vote for it. I attribute 80 percent of my progress to it. If you want to write your personal mission statement, visit my blog and follow the guidance:

www.expandbeyondyourself.com/how-to-write-personal-mission-statement/

---

[1] *7 Habits of Highly Effective People* by Stephen R. Covey

All of the above examples are just that—examples. Those disciplines worked well in my case but won't necessarily be as effective for you. Don't restrict yourself to just them. You will find your way to discover your own unique methods to observe your self-talk, your internal interpretation of the events from the outside world.

Why all this hassle with self-examination? Well, apart from it being indicated as a success factor by numerous sages, for this kind of job—developing your personal philosophy—you must realize what parts of your present worldview hinder your progress. You want to remodel yourself. In order to do that you need to know what your "shape" is right now. Transforming your mental constitution is very similar to character-forming disciplines the Stoics practiced. The word "character" comes from the Greek word meaning to chisel or the mark left by a chisel. A chisel is a steel tool used for making a sculpture out of hard or difficult material, like granite. You are like an unformed clod of matter that needs chiseling to bring out the outstanding sculpture hidden inside. The excess matter must be discarded, chiseled out to reveal the statue inside. To do that, you need to make an internal inventory.

Does it mean that you will have to stop being yourself and transform into someone else? In a way, yes. But it's you who consciously determines what to choose and—most important in this phase—what to discard from your current philosophy.

It's not New Age stuff. Benjamin Franklin did something similar, which also gives some consideration to the importance of habits. You can check it out here:

http://www.gutenberg.org/files/20203/20203-h/20203-h.htm#IX

The master sculptor doesn't focus very much on which piece of excess matter to discard. He has a vision of what is hidden in the clay and he steadily aims to materialize this vision. Benjamin Franklin did the same by defining the virtues he wanted to master. You just need to be aware that some parts of your present constitution are disturbing. However, your main task is to form a new personal philosophy, not to analyze the old one.

Benjamin Franklin is worth mimicking. Focus on what you want to achieve. List all of those traits and goals. Form appropriate habits to achieve them. Build new healthy elements of your personal philosophy.

Action Items:

- *Keep a journal as your main indicator of how serious you are about adjusting your personal philosophy.*
- *Create and make a habit of using a personal mission statement.*
- *Read the fragment of Benjamin Franklin's autobiography and copy his process.*

The Company You Keep

"You are the average of the five people you spend the most time with."

— Jim Rohn

In the chapter *Analyze Your Data Sources*, I dwelt on how to incorporate new data sources into your life. In the previous chapter, I pointed out journaling as a great habit for self-analysis to track and change your internal interpretation of events and experiences. You need the habits to also change your social environment. New data sources may offer opportunities to meet new people. The host of the podcast you start to listen to, the owner of a blog you start to follow, their followers—all of them are potential new buddies. I encourage you to look for new acquaintances online. It's not true that online relationships are *all* impersonal and superficial. They tend to be that, but they can be so much more.

About a year ago, I joined "Pat's First Kindle Book" on Facebook. It's a huge group of indie authors who share not only tips and tricks, but also encourage and cheer each other. I learned a lot there, but I also got new business connections, including the editor of a couple of my books, who also became my accountability partner.

Social media can be addictive, so beware. While the Transformation Contest was running, I spent an hour a day reading my friends' entries and commenting on them. But social media is also very handy in developing habits. You can set the reminder to log onto Facebook at 9 p.m. and set the timer to spend just fifteen minutes on it. You don't have such flexibility with one-on-one interactions.

Once you change the kind of information you absorb, the kind of people you interact with, and your internal interpretation of your experiences, your actions will change too. To accelerate this process, you should consciously look for new experiences. Start a new activity, preferably involving new people, and you will attain the change of all the three basic elements of personal philosophy at once. For me, such an activity was joining the Transformational Contest. There I met people from other continents and cultures with different sexual orientations and religious beliefs, an amazing mix of individuals I wouldn't have met in the offline world. I started a new activity, journaling (up until the contest, I had only a gratitude diary for my wife). And the nature of this activity made me mindful of my internal interpreter. I was describing my actions and motives. I was giving my opinions and advice to the other contestants.

It accelerated my progress many fold, but I saw it only in hindsight. And I did it all on a whim—"*Why not join the online contest, it can be fun, it can be useful.*" You can design your accelerator consciously, knowing which elements to seek.

Whatever activity you choose for gaining new experiences, I strongly encourage you to socialize with new people. Humans are the most unpredictable creatures on the planet. They bring the indeterminism factor into your life like nothing else.

Action Items:

- *Carefully choose an online community that shares your passion and values.*
- *Join such a community, interact there daily, and track your time spent (beware of a social media addiction).*

Learn from Others

"If you want to be successful, find someone who has achieved the results you want and copy what they do and you'll achieve the same results."

— Tony Robbins

Even the most successful philosophy that belongs to someone else is not able to transform *your* life. It can be seen throughout history. Sages and teachers tried to pass their wisdom to others, but without much success. We had only one Socrates and one Jim Rohn. Certainly, there were fewer successful stories out of Jim Rohn's seminars and programs than attendants and listeners. Some very successful individuals like Tony Robbins, Darren Hardy, and Jeff Olson credit much of their success to Rohn's lessons, but they found their unique ways to apply those lessons.

Nonetheless, there are many universal elements in the personal philosophies of successful people. A few of them have already been pointed out in this book. You don't have to reinvent the wheel. If so many people have so many beliefs and ideas in common, it is possible to adopt them. The word "adopt" fits here. Those foreign, external elements of philosophy may be used by you only when you take ownership of them. You cannot just learn them; you must *know* that they are *true*. Only then is your brain appropriately hypnotized to utilize them.

You may be afraid that adopting these beliefs and developing these traits will turn you into some kind of corporate clone and you'll lose your uniqueness. It's not a valid fear. Compare any half a dozen successful people you know—great entrepreneurs, artists, scientists, sportsmen, or sages. They may have a core of common beliefs, they may have the same traits, but each of them is different from the other. It's not those success blocks themselves, but how you merge them into your philosophy that will lead you to your success. You can take perseverance, integrity, courage, and decisiveness and mix them in proportions unique to you. You take the common elements and create an uncommon formula out of them. *Your own* success formula. You just consciously do what was done to you on the subconscious level: digest, analyze, and discard or keep all the data inputs. The ones you keep shape your internal constitution.

As a kid, you didn't analyze your parents' teachings very much, you just accepted them. In a normal family, Mom and Dad are not just figures of authority. They are the most loved and trusted people in the whole world. You mimicked them and absorbed their philosophies by osmosis, just living with them day by day. You probably know the saying, "Do as I say, not as I do." If you have your own kids, you know what BS this is. You certainly know it if your parents ever tried to use it against you.

You didn't need sermons to inherit behavior from your parents. I can't recall a single conversation with my dad about the value of equanimity. When I try, my mind is totally blank. But I can recall no more than half a dozen cases when he lost his cool. I identified with my wonderful dad in my childhood, so equanimity is a part of me. My sisters identified with my more dynamic mom and equanimity is quite foreign for them (Funny, most of the instances when my dad lost his temper involved kicking discussions with my mom).

That's the natural process of forming your system for conduct of life. You observe what's going on around you (peppy mom, calm dad), interpret that data (I want to be like dad, so I'll be tranquil), and act according to the results of your analysis.

I'm the most religious person in my family. When I was seventeen, I found a church community and felt a calling to join it. Theoretically, I was a Christian, a Catholic, but I didn't really feel it. I was learning almost everything from scratch—prayers, reading the Bible, and so on. I inherited this very weak bond with God from my parents. I remember when I was trying to explain my conversion to my mom, she said something like, "Yes, I know, God is somewhere far away, and we are here on our own."

That was her personal philosophy regarding religion and spiritual life. With such a belief system, it's not strange she didn't pass faith on to me. You cannot give something you don't have. With this conviction, she didn't pray. Why should she? God was far away and left her on her own. In her mind, it was like trying to be heard by shouting through the ocean. Hopeless.

My sisters also inherited our mother's philosophy, more or less. They hadn't the strong experience I had (joining a church community) to change or challenge their worldview. My personal philosophy shifted a bit with my church community experience. And I not only think but act differently than my relatives in the realm of religion.

You can absolutely use the same process of attitude osmosis, this time through the use of intellect, which will accelerate the whole process. And it's the *only* way it can be done. New elements of philosophy, new ideas, new attitudes must come through the guard you have put up around you. They must be let in; they can't conquer you. Your internal fortress is your last stronghold. It's your essence. Your whole being stems from it. New ideas can only be allowed in and adopted as a part of its walls. If they conquer you by force, they will triumph only on the smoky ruins of your old self. Such subjugation equals madness.

That's one of the reasons you resist change and especially the change in your internal composure regarding your personal philosophy. You are stable and you don't want to get mad.

Knowledge Items:

– *Even the most successful philosophy belonging to someone else is not able to transform your life.*

– *Attitude osmosis is a natural process, which you can accelerate through the use of intellect.*

Choosing New Beliefs

"Ignorance is not bliss."

— Jim Rohn

A few months ago, my friend asked me how I maintain my inhuman consistency. I replied via her blog post and while writing it, I realized that many beliefs have "sneaked" into my personal philosophy. I didn't plan it that way. It just happened because I changed my data sources, met new people, and worked hard on my spiritual and personal development, which led to a drastic transformation in the internal interpretation of my experiences.

Starting from that blog post, I did reverse engineering to discover how my personal philosophy had transmuted. It led me to writing this book. I believe you can have more control over this process than I had. That's why I'll provide you with dozens of pieces of successful people's philosophies. You can absorb them all or just the chosen ones. You can adopt them one by one or all at once (if possible). Or you can just let the natural process of philosophy osmosis change your worldview the way mine has changed: by consciously choosing who you interact with, what you read, watch, and listen to, and by journaling.

Knowing these successful bits in advance will accelerate your progress. They are not universally right; they are just most common among people who have achieved a lot in their lives. When you read biographies of entrepreneurs or books written by them, you recognize this effortlessly. They don't unanimously eulogize perseverance, integrity, courage, or decisiveness, but the *majority* of them do. So those blocks are not universal for success, but they are a close approximation of a universal success philosophy. This is indicated by a multitude of successful individuals over thousands of years, and across different cultural backgrounds. Quite solid evidence if you ask me.

It's unlikely that you can craft your own philosophy with some totally new approach not based on those success blocks. Too many people utilized them with great effect to ignore them. They are common simply because they work. They use the laws that govern the material world, spiritual world, and human society.

Some of those philosophy pieces may be not suitable for you. Breaking relationships in the name of progress is not for me, for example. But *most* of them are good for you, because they are the distilled wisdom of thousands of people who applied them successfully. Don't dismiss them too readily. Regard them carefully, weigh your options rigorously, and discard them only after thoughtful consideration. Because some of them *should* be discarded by you. A universal formula for success doesn't exist or we would all already be successful. You need to find your own path, in accordance with your deepest values, beliefs, and life experiences. If something just doesn't feel right for you, no matter how you wrap your mind around the concept, don't use it. Don't try to force the change. Force causes resistance.

The grand goal is to rebuild your personal philosophy. The immediate one is to make those chosen elements a part of it. You can only make that happen if they are true for *you*. Borrowing them won't cut the mustard. You must adopt them. However, if you go through the list and discard most of the elements—"that's stupid," "oh, it can't be the truth," "that sounds like naive thinking," "it's not like me," "that surely won't work in my case"—beware! It may be just your old, messy philosophy in action. Part of personal philosophy is interpretation. You already have some interpretation subroutines established. Considering that the results you get in life are far from perfect, it is quite possible that those subroutines are far from perfect too. Be mindful of this fact.

Using those success blocks doesn't automatically make you a success. It just increases your chances significantly. You can meticulously develop perseverance, determination, integrity, and resourcefulness, but ignore how important tracking is for success and steadily head in the wrong direction for years.

Those statements don't have to feel like dogma. Well, very likely they don't, if they aren't part of your recent philosophy now. However, if they feel true enough for you to give them a chance, that's enough. If a given sentence sounds to you like utter hogwash, don't try to accommodate it into your worldview right now. The internal resistance caused by cognitive incongruence will be too high to profit from this "success rule." You will spend more energy on adopting this belief or trait than receiving it in the form of results. Wait. Adopt other beliefs. Work on your input sources and interpretation. Go back to the list in a month or six months and examine your attitude once again.

Another handy criteria is, "Do I really want to make it part of me for the rest of my life?" Your personal philosophy is really part of you, something at your core that determines who you become and what actions you undertake. When you let some new piece of philosophy into your internal fortress, it will affect your life in a very serious way going forward. It will probably stay with you for the rest of your life. So, don't just choose something that sounds cool. Pick up only those blocks from the list that you feel may be integrated with your being without long-term damage.

"What, then, will anyone gain by winning the whole world and forfeiting his life?"

- Mt. 16:26

The list in the following chapter is an appendix to this book. There is more than one way to skin a cat, but there are only a handful that are most effective. If you are going to achieve success in any area, you are bound to be equipped with traits and beliefs in common with the successful people known throughout history.

Don't rush the process of picking and adopting these "success blocks." The biggest mistake you can make is to skim through them and pick them more or less at random. You mark this activity as done and never go back to the exercise. It's a mistake I made over and over again with some potentially useful personal development stuff. I know a guy who claims that *Awaken the Giant Within* by Tony Robbins has changed his life, to the point where he earns seven figures and is very happy with his life. I read the same book about eighteen years ago and I'm (sadly) no millionaire. I enjoyed the book a lot and I made some immediate changes in my life because of it. But I remember that each time there was some exercise in the book I skipped "for later" (read: never) or did it hastily, without much reflection. My life didn't transform then and the changes I introduced fizzled out in less than a year.

Your horizon will expand with the development of your personal philosophy. You will open up to new ideas and concepts. Don't be afraid to refer to this list again and again. Come back to it in a week, a month, or a year and you will find other nuggets hidden there, as your perspective will shift.

If your current philosophy stands in the way of accepting these bits of wisdom, take a step back and work on expanding the more "technical" aspects of changing your philosophy—using new data sources and meeting new people. As long as you persist, the shift in your perspective is unavoidable. These disciplines must bear fruit. It's the law of nature.

Action items:

— *Go mindfully through the success blocks enumerated in the next chapter and pick some you would like to incorporate in your life.*

- *Find a way to refer to them every day (stick them to your fridge, record them and listen to them on your mobile phone, ruminate on them in your journal, etc.)*
- *If you don't find the list below compelling, go through the quotes of a few successful people you admire and pick several of their "success blocks." Refer to them daily.*

Philosopher's Stepping Stones

Time

Success is a process, not a destination.

You are bound to work for the rest of your life. Even if you reach a certain level of success, the world won't stop at that place.

People are incapable of enjoying the same state for an extended period of time.

Time is your only asset; anything else is just a function of time.

Every action gives results; sometimes it's experience, sometimes feedback, sometimes the output you desired. It's never in vain.

Your body will accompany you to the end.

You will die.

You will live in the memory of others.

The fruits of your work may serve others long after you are dead.

Each of your past experiences may be used to your advantage; each of them helped to shape who you are now.

You don't know your hour. Use each minute to its fullest.

Work on your important goals every day.

You can only act now; the past is settled, the future is still undefined.

Your past is not equal to your future.

You can do only one thing at a time; choose wisely which one.

Discipline is choosing between what you want now and what you want most.

People

Providing value is at the core of being rewarded; providing value to people is the most profitable.

People are the most important; respect them, serve them, love them.

Your family is a microcosm and reflects your inner world and your potential achievements in wider society.

Humans are interconnected.

As long as you feel you are serving others, you will do the job well.

Do to others what you would like to be done to you.

Every human is a child of God.

Every human is your brother or sister.

Who you become is more important than what you have.

Who someone else is, is more important than what he has.

Real success doesn't happen at the expense of others.

When a man works, he not only alters things and society, he develops himself as well. He learns much, he cultivates his resources, he goes outside of himself and beyond himself. Rightly understood, this kind of growth is of greater value than any external riches that can be garnered. A man is more precious for what he is than for what he has.

Character

Courage is not the absence of fear; it's acting against the fear.

You can, you should, and if you're brave enough to start, you will.

You should only fear that you won't measure up to your standards.

A comfort zone is a comfort pit.

Growth costs and hurts. The price of staying in place is exponentially higher.

If you think you have all the answers, you'd better look for different questions.

Your habits determine your net worth.

The wicked people and fools both get what they deserve. The fools get it earlier.

Ask the questions.

If you seek, you will find.

Do what you say you are going to do.

Don't lie.

Keep your promises.

Walk your talk.

Keep your body in good shape; it's your support system.

Smile at everybody and everywhere.

If you quit, you won't reach your goal.

The only failure is in not trying.

When your philosophy is right, then your consistency is right, too.

Do it until you achieve it.

Not everything is attainable. But nothing is attainable when you do nothing.

The patient man can always afford to wait.

You won't break if you bend.

Spirituality

If you don't believe in something beyond the matter, you are limiting yourself to "just" the human level.

Be grateful for everything.

Practice gratitude.

Only love is rewarded in Heaven.

You don't belong to yourself. You are created.

Your role is to develop your humanity to the highest standards you are capable of.

Development requires attention to the spiritual life, a serious consideration of the experiences of trust in God, spiritual fellowship in Christ, reliance upon God's providence and mercy, love and forgiveness, self-denial, acceptance of others, justice and peace.

The social order and its development must invariably work to the benefit of the human if the disposition of affairs is to be subordinate to the personal realm and not to the contrary.

Attitude

You are responsible for everything in your life.

Accept that you will be learning for the rest of your life.

Keep a journal.

I don't feel the best every day, but I'm gonna bring the best.

Guard your speech.

Read books.

Learn continually.

Mind over matter.

Imagination is everything. It is the preview of life's coming attractions.

Dream, visualize, use a vision board.

Write down your goals.

Tracking is the foundation of growth.

To increase your chances of success, double your ratio of failures.

Motivation doesn't last. That's why it's recommended daily.

Motivation is what gets you started. Habit is what keeps you going.

Your personal philosophy is the greatest determining factor in how your life works out.

Progress is your duty.

Follow the right people.

Mimic successful people.

You can hedge. Just think it over twice.

Apply Your New Philosophy

"Numbers are the name of the game."

— Jim Rohn

You don't need more details or more knowledge to develop your personal philosophy. You need to start implementing what you've learned or just refreshed in your mind. I could go into more detailed instructions, but it would be highly repetitive and it's already insistent enough. Besides, all the instructions won't help much if you don't apply them. You are the main architect of your personal philosophy. You need to decide where to start and with what level of intensity. You must choose success blocks appropriate to your situation. So, no more preaching on my part, just a quick rehearsal.

Why work on your personal philosophy?

Because it determines almost every output in your life. No school, no trainer, no coach, no book, no personal development program, no info product can transform your life without your cooperation. Unfortunately, this factor seems to be overlooked. Academies, coaches, and gurus are focused far too much on providing an incentive to pay them rather than giving you an incentive to get results. They give promises and 30-day guarantees for your revolution, but fail to supervise the process of implementing this revolution.

But once you develop the right personal philosophy, you will get more clarity about whether or not any given program is for you, whether or not you are willing to pay the price in time investment and sacrifices, not just in money. And you will be able to implement almost anything you decide is worth pursuing.

You can change and you can change rapidly, but it will cost you. You can revolutionize your personal philosophy quickly, but in order to do it you need to revolutionize your life. Your current philosophy has been forming for years; you need extraordinary measures to rebuild it quickly. But you can examine yourself, and target traits, concepts and beliefs that stand in your way. Then you can chisel away at them and develop good routines one by one. You will accelerate the natural process of reshaping your philosophy by applying your awareness, attention, and focus.

Start by changing your data sources. Examine the inputs you are exposed to in your everyday life. Check how much time you spend watching TV and on YouTube. Check the social media you use. How much do you read and what kind of materials. Are they books, magazines, or short stories? What kind of books—pop fiction or non-fiction? And so on.

Numbers are very tangible, not some woo-woo talk about philosophy, interpretation, and a higher purpose. They are technical, mechanical, something your conscious secular mind can grasp. You can easily introduce and track your disciplines regarding data sources. Read ten pages of a self-help book a day; listen to a single podcast episode while commuting; stop watching TV news altogether; watch a classic movie once per week; follow a new blog and read one post a day; join a group on social media and interact there five minutes a day. It's all easy to do, easy not to do, and easy to track. It's easy to build new habits around these activities.

I guarantee that if you stick to your new routine for an extended period of time, you will change. If you start a daily activity, give yourself at least 100 days to notice this change. When starting a weekly one, be prepared to continue it for the next couple of years.

The internal interpretation of facts (external data) and your experiences (external data plus your emotions) is less tangible. It is also more important. You can bombard yourself with different messages, but if you dismiss all of them with an incorrect interpretation, you won't get any results; that's the example of reaction to your sustained action. That way you nullify the effect of the law of small errors and consistent discipline. A mere change in what kind of information you consume may be useless if you proactively sabotage those messages.

The best indication that your interpretation is not working against you is that you regard new elements of your personal philosophy as true. Once they are true in your mind and in your soul, you don't have to worry about consciously cultivating them.

You need to change in order to change your results. That's why change in both the sources and quality of information you habitually absorb is necessary. That's why your internal interpretation, your self-talk, must change. It's not a matter of learning and applying some fancy technique that will help you lose weight, save more money, get more friends, or whatever else you are after. All the knowledge and skills you possess are dependent on your personal philosophy. Without the change in philosophy, you may experience some success with those new techniques, but then the yo-yo effect will kick in. You will be back to your starting position.

Believe in Yourself

"If anyone else has done it, you can do it, and if someone else hasn't done it, you can do it first."

— Jeremy Frandsen's grandma

The facts are that 80 percent of people are not satisfied with their lives. About 15 percent don't accept their situation and struggle to squeeze more out of their lives. And only about 5 percent reach their dreams.

Whatever data sets you examine, this distribution is clear. I researched only the data of multi-level marketing (MLM) companies and online ventures. But the data confirmed the gut feeling we all have: success is not common. Even if you live in Beverly Hills, if you open your eyes, you will notice that, yes, there are a lot of mansions around, but there is also an army of drivers, bodyguards, gardeners, and maids. The proportions are the same.

To achieve success, you must not only *do* what the top 5 percent does, you must *think* the way they do. Adopting someone else's beliefs is not a small feat, otherwise the world would be full of Einsteins and Bob Proctors. But if you utilize the natural process of reshaping your worldview, which takes place every minute in your head, the change in your mindset is possible and much easier to attain.

There are other factors indicated as the philosopher's stone of success. Some say that confidence is the mysterious ingredient. Others, and not just small fish, but big figures like Thomas Edison or John D. Rockefeller, say it's perseverance. I say it's those traits and a bunch of others, like wisdom and flexibility. They are important but they are all secondary to your system for conduct of life. Your personal philosophy determines what level of confidence, perseverance, or flexibility is characterizing you. When you adopt the right beliefs and make them your own, you can develop the above-mentioned traits to the levels that characterize successful people.

Perseverance comes from personal philosophy. I was quite persistent before my life transition. For example, I have been doing pushups every single day for about four years. But since I introduced some changes in my philosophy I also write, do pull-ups, eat veggies and fruits, study the Bible, read books written by saints, look at my vision board, repeat my personal mission statement, practice speed reading, keep journals, pray with my kids, and do a few more things on daily basis. Once I accepted the law of small errors and consistent disciplines as true, I had no problems with perseverance.

All I needed to do was to start a new activity and track the results. As long as I kept doing this new thing, the results were unavoidable. I observed it in several different areas of my life, which led me to the belief that it's universal for every human activity. That's why I stuck with my writing.

I was writing for eight months and earned less than $80. Anyone with the wrong personal philosophy would have given up. His flawed philosophy would have justified quitting: "Well, this clearly doesn't work, so you need to find another path," or "Hard work is overhyped. Sit down and enjoy your day instead of working like crazy." But I continued and you read my seventh book.

Everything is possible with the help of the right personal philosophy. Everything that has ever happened, happened because of someone's philosophy—Lech Walesa's, Albert Einstein's, Nelson Mandela's, Martin Luther King's, Gustav Eiffel's.

And it is so easy to remodel your philosophy! You just improve the natural process you are already using. It's not complicated. All you need to do at the beginning is to open your mind a bit and read, listen to, and watch different things than you did previously. Do it consistently and the transformation will take place.

It is doable. It happens all the time. Most people manage to discard or dismiss all the ideas that challenge their status quo and stay the same...today. Tomorrow they will receive new inputs and another chance to shift their personal philosophy.

You may still be doubtful about whether you can do it. The only answer I have is that if I can do it, anyone can. I was content with my system for conduct of life. I graduated from university, my career was steadily progressing, my kids were growing healthy, life wasn't bad. I spent more than ten years without reading a single personal development book. What for? I "knew" that it was all "rubbish," wishful thinking, and opium for the masses. It couldn't work in my life. I tried it and I "knew" it.

But then my life became stale. I was fired from my job and in the new one, my salary didn't grow very fast. My wife started to dream about a house and we were in no position to buy one. My savings weren't increasing at all. I gained some weight. Life wasn't cozy anymore. Then I read *The Slight Edge* and decided to give its philosophy a try. I didn't suddenly get woo-woo, believing in the Law of Attraction or mumbling affirmations all day long. I just changed the books I read and started to listen to personal development audio materials. For almost three months I did nothing more.

Once I wrote my personal mission statement in November 2012, things started to move faster. I created my first blog, I made new online acquaintances, I wrote my first book. Two years later here I am not quite recognizing myself. My personal philosophy has transformed dramatically. I think differently and act differently.

And there are tangible results of those philosophy changes in my life. Concrete outputs. Seven books published. Thousands of copies sold. Hundreds of mails to/from my readers. Dozens of blog posts published and the traffic to my blog has increased. People follow me! That's incredible! I have friends who read my entries on Lift every day. Who am I to be looked up to? But it all happened.

Your personal philosophy is an integral part of you. It will be with you as long as you breathe. Don't neglect to work on it because your life didn't quite work out as you dreamed it would. Being low in your life is a great starting point for transformation. You don't have much to lose. You have a lot to gain. You are frustrated to the point that you are willing to change and get out of your comfort pit.

One belief I got out of my transformation is that it is much better to change before you have to. Transform yourself because you want to have a better life, not because you have to escape the smoking ruins of your old one. Don't just react; act in advance. Be prepared for whatever the future will bring. Start now. Right this minute. Before you put down this book, plan. Decide which single tiny discipline you will practice: Reading specific kinds of books? Reading a professional periodical? Following a few blogs? Subscribing to a useful YouTube channel?

Make it a consistent discipline. Practice it daily. Do it day after day, week after week, month after month. Consistency equals lasting results. Consistency builds momentum. Do something every day and you are harnessing the law of nature to work for you.

Never give up. Consider all of your small failures as feedback loops. Learn from them. Track your progress. Whatever discipline you start you need to simultaneously start the tracking process. Describe it in a measurable rate. Ten minutes or ten pages. One podcast episode, one video or fifteen minutes of them. One chapter of the Bible. Two financial articles from a business magazine. A couple of phone calls. Five minutes in an online community. Only if you track those seemingly trifling activities can you observe your lapses and their reasons. Feed your mind with facts; don't let it fight you with imaginary pictures and judgments.

That's it. I wish you determination, consistency, and resolve. You don't need anything more to succeed. Go and work on your philosopher's stone. From now on, begin turning everything you touch—relationships, health, finances, parenting, education—into gold.

Godspeed!

Bonus Section: 20 Activities to Get You Started

Data sources:

1. Listen to one podcast episode.
2. Listen to audio book for at least ten minutes.
3. Watch one video on a specialized YouTube channel.
4. Watch one TED talk.
5. Read one chapter of the Bible (or The Holy Scripture of your religion; or read it for five minutes).
6. Read ten (or just two) pages of a good book (or read for ten minutes).
7. Read a single specialized blog post.
8. Read a single random blog post (just type an interesting topic into Google).
9. Read one article from a professional magazine.

Interpretation:

10. Join and start using Lift (interactions bonus: follow other people's entries and comment on them).
11. Answer one insightful question a day (the best way: on paper).
12. Keep a gratitude journal.
13. Start a blog and work on it every day (not necessarily post daily, just make working on your blog a part of your routine).
14. Keep a journal.
15. Pray or meditate for five minutes.

Interactions:

16. Spend ten minutes in an online community.
17. Text a friend (or a few of them).
18. Write a blog comment.
19. Join Twitter and do one of the following: retweet a single message, follow one new person, send a message to one person.
20. Make a phone call (or two, or three).

Free Gift for You

Thanks for reading all the way to the end. If you made it this far, you must have liked it! I really appreciate having people all over the world take interest in the thoughts, ideas, research, and words that I share in my books. I appreciate it so much that I invite you to visit www.michalzone.com, where you can register to receive all of my future releases absolutely free. You won't receive any annoying emails or product offers or anything distasteful by being subscribed to my mailing list. This is purely an invite to receive my future book releases for free as a way of saying thanks to you for taking a sincere interest in my work. Once again, that's www.michalzone.com

A Small Favor

I want to ask a favor of you. If you have found value in this book, please take a moment and share your opinion with the world. Just let me know what you learned and how it affected you in a positive way. Your reviews help me to positively change the lives of others. Thank you!

About the Author

I'm Michal Stawicki and I live in Poland, Europe. I've been married for over twelve years and am the father of two boys and one girl. I work full time in the IT industry, and recently, I've become an author. My passions are transparency, integrity, and progress.

In August 2012, I read a book called *The Slight Edge* by Jeff Olson. It took me a whole month to start implementing ideas from this book. That led me to reading numerous other books on personal development, some effective, some not so much. I took a look at myself and decided this was one person who could surely use some development.

In November of 2012, I created my personal mission statement; I consider it the real starting point of my progress. Over several months' time, I applied numerous self-help concepts and started building inspiring results: I lost some weight, greatly increased my savings, built new skills, and got rid of bad habits while developing better ones.

I'm very pragmatic, a down-to-earth person. I favor utilitarian, bottom-line results over pure artistry. Despite the ridiculous language, however, I found there is value in the "hokey-pokey visualization" stuff and I now see it as my mission to share what I have learned.

My books are not abstract. I avoid going mystical as much as possible. I don't believe that pure theory is what we need in order to change our lives; the Internet age has proven this quite clearly. What you will find in my books are:

- Detailed techniques and methods describing how you can improve your skills and drive results in specific areas of your life
- Real life examples
- Personal stories

So, whether you are completely new to personal development or have been crazy about the Law of Attraction for years, if you are looking for concrete strategies, you will find them in my books. My writing shows that I am a relatable, ordinary guy and not some ivory tower guru.

Made in the USA
Lexington, KY
06 October 2016